FAMILY
Personalities

David Field

343-1391

HARVEST HOUSE PUBLISHERS
Eugene, Oregon 97402

Except where otherwise indicated, all Scripture quotations in this book are taken from the Holy Bible, New International Version, Copyright © 1973, 1978, 1984 International Bible Society. Used by permission.

FAMILY PERSONALITIES

Copyright © 1988 by David Field
Published by Harvest House Publishers
Eugene, Oregon 97402

Library of Congress Cataloging-in-Publication Data

Field, David, 1944-
    Family personalities.

      1. Family—Psychological aspects.   2. Parent and child.   3. Family—Religious life.   I. Title.
HQ518.F48   1988   306.8'5   87-82259
ISBN   0-89081-627-1

Printed in the United States of America.

Dedicated to my three-generational family—
My parents, Gene and Jo Ann Field
My wife's parents, Lon and Ruth Setser
My wife, Lonna
My children, Tory, Jonathan and Dana

Contents

Appendix

Helpful Source Materials

Preface

Many adults are in the unique position of being a parent and a child at the same time. On one side we have our families of origin into which we were born. On the other side we have our present families consisting of the spouses we have chosen and the children we have borne.

How do we respond to the demands of this dual role? I am convinced we will do a better job with our marriages and children as we maintain an active relationship with our parents and deal with the difficulties of the past.

This book is the result of countless hours I have spent helping patients put their families of origin in perspective. For many, a proper view of their family past has proved to be an integral part of living more successfully today. They are more confident and fulfilled in their relationships with their parents. I share these thoughts as a professional but I also speak as an adult child who has learned to enjoy both of my families. Through these chapters let us encourage one another in our God-given family opportunities.

David Field
Clearwater, Florida

The
Three-Generational
Family

– 1 –

The Three-Generational Family

Sarah gripped her screaming three-year-old boy by the arm and continued spanking him as she marched him up the stairs. When they reached the child's room, she firmly set him on his bed, then left, slamming the door behind her. "I must get control of myself," she thought. "Why do I keep losing my temper over my son whom I love?"

Charlie, a confused 39-year-old man, was sitting in my office. Recently he'd sold his business for a large profit. He had two delightful children, and a wife who enjoyed his company and supported him in all his efforts. "Everything should be right for me," he said, "but in the last six months I've had this vague sense of loss. I'm not as motivated as I used to be. I don't seem to care about anything. I have trouble going to my new office. I can't understand why I'm feeling like this."

Doreen knew she wasn't perfect, but she'd had it with her husband. Ever since they had married, she had worked hard while he aimlessly shifted from job to job. The only reason they had survived was because of continued help from his parents. Now, during the last six months, he had become reclusive—not talking to her, their kids, or anyone. Doreen couldn't understand his behavior. After all, he'd enjoyed many more advantages in life. "What's his problem?" she asked me.

Christy couldn't believe that she was being treated so badly by her 17-year-old daughter. "I've done just about everything you can do for that kid. Now she won't give me the time of day, except when she wants me to put gas in the car so she can run around with friends I don't approve of. I don't know what I can do. If I took the car away from her, she would hate me forever. I guess I'll just put up with it until she leaves for college. Then maybe things will settle down."

Lawrence told me how he would agitate an animal until it bit or scratched him. Then he would turn on the animal and beat it. He had been married three times and his most recent wife had left him complaining about threats of violence. He asked me, "How come I continue to hurt the people I love?"

The Impact of the Family Past

Each of these people, without consciously recognizing it, was acting or reacting according to input they received as children from their parents. Each of them found help when they confronted issues that were rooted in their childhood family. It's true: The family from which you came continues to affect you every day of your adult life. Some people ignore this fact; others overemphasize it. But regardless of the individual reaction, the genetic code of the family past works its way out through our present relationships in life.

Our present lives are attached to our previous families as if by an umbilical cord. Our behavior and thoughts, our attitudes and reactions, and our values and beliefs are all linked to the family from which we came. Our conscious and unconscious actions and attitudes are tied to what I call our families of origin.

The family of origin is the home in which you were raised. For some that home is very easy to identify. You had two parents and grew up with one or more siblings, or as an only child. But for others the family of origin is more difficult to identify because your parents did not stay together. You may have had one or more stepparents, lived with other family members, or been a foster child. But by and large your family of origin is that family group you lived in most of the time as a child. If you were adopted at a young age, your family of origin is the adoptive family in which you grew up.

As a marriage and family therapist, I've been trained to work with people from a relationship perspective. My primary job is to assist people with their interpersonal relationships. I assess the actions and reactions of people in relationship to others, and help them adjust their interpersonal exchanges so they will be more effective with one another. My job is not so much to change people's minds as it is to help them adjust their relationships.

But there's more to my work than just trying to bandage broken relationships. It goes back to my second year in college when I was introduced to the claims of Jesus Christ, confessed my sins, and believed in Him as my Savior. Since then my purpose has been to help, and bring hope, to hurting people. My cause is the family—the bedrock social structure of society.

It's this training, my years of counseling, and my cause that lead me to talk about family personalities. In so many cases of marital and family difficulty, I invariably find that there is a correlation between what is happening in the present generation and what has happened in the previous generation, or the family of origin. Often in discovering and understanding the dynamics of the family of origin, we become more effective in resolving today's relational conflicts.

The Adult Child:
Caught in the Middle
Between Two Families

This book is written to you, the adult child who needs to learn about and work through the effects of his or her family of origin. You've likely been married 10 to 25 years. Most of you have experienced some slippage in the vitality of your marriage relationship. Perhaps there's some distance between you and your spouse. You also have some questions about your relationship with your surviving parents. And certainly those young children of yours present some real challenges. You probably feel just a little strung out.

As the diagram shows, you are right in the middle. You feel stretched as the adult child, trying to balance a relationship with your parents, your spouse, and your children. How do you do it and still maintain some degree of individuality? With regard to your parents you are probably dealing with their anticipated retirement, aging years, and possibly their deaths. In regard to your adolescents, you are dealing with the ambivalence of their part-child/part-adult development, the process of their leaving home, and possibly anxiety about their future. On the one hand you may want them to leave; on the other hand you feel some real anxiety about it.

This is a book about adult children and their relationships with their parents, both past and present. It's a book with a goal: To help you gain understanding about your relationship with your parents so you will be more effective in dealing with your spouse and your children, and be more at peace with yourself.

No doubt you're reading this book because you have questions about your relationship with your parents. You may have suffered so many negative experiences that your relationship with them is "stuck." This is a book to help you get "unstuck." As you understand some of the things that happened to you as a child, you can prevent duplicating the same mistakes with your own children. It's never too late to understand your family of origin and make some changes, even if your children are getting ready to leave home.

What about the people I introduced at the beginning of this chapter? Sarah, who was spanking her child, finally learned to exercise control over her behavior and reduce the amount of anger that she was feeling. She was helped immensely, not just by learning new parenting techniques, but by dealing with some lifelong antagonism and frustration toward her father. He had spanked her in the same way she spanked her son—impulsively, with overreaction. It was as if she were replaying the scenes she experienced as a child.

As for Charlie, the 39-year-old man who felt no motivation, his problem was linked to the death of his father six months earlier. In many respects, the death was a relief to Charlie. His parents were divorced when he was young and his dad had never been very good at supporting him or coming to see him. Charlie's dad had been a leech, an embarrassment, a disappointment, and a source of hurt and pain. Charlie felt more disgust for his father than anything else, but there was nothing he could do to disown him. His death brought the relationship to a close, but did not end the history of the relationship which Charlie still carried. Once he worked through the feelings he had toward his father, his depression lifted and his direction returned.

It was the same with the other situations. Doreen, Christy, and Lawrence gained valuable insight into their current relationships by understanding and resolving the personalities of their families of origin. Insight alone, of course, didn't solve their present problems. However, it was an important first step. Once they understood why they were acting a certain way, they were free to take corrective action.

It doesn't matter whether the relationship you had with your parents was mild or traumatic. I have rarely run into an adult child who has not needed, at one time or another, to resolve issues with his parents. Sometimes that means a conversation with Mom or Dad or both. Sometimes it means just getting it straight from our own perspective. *Family Personalities* will help you, the adult child, understand your family of origin and your current behavior and feelings, and help you become a peer to your parents and truly honor them.

Family
Personalities

– 2 –

Family Personalities

On several occasions my wife Lonna and I have talked together about our relationships with our parents. We've compared and contrasted their parenting styles. We've discussed how each couple gets along as husband and wife. Since the beginning of our marriage, we have realized how different our childhood homes were. We grew up with dissimilar parenting styles and each of us responded differently to our parents. There were certain methods and attitudes our parents employed that we liked and others that we disliked.

Lonna and I found that leaving our parents' homes and joining together in marriage did not mean leaving behind the personality, habits, values, and behavior style of our families of origin. We still play out, in our marriage and our parenting, some of the habits and patterns that we knew as children. For example, Lonna's parenting style is confrontive, while I prefer to reason and avoid conflict with our children. Our different parenting styles are reflective of the parenting styles in our respective families of origin.

A Confrontation of Personalities

Recently, an incident with one of our children led to a confrontation between Lonna and me. Lonna raised an issue with our child and before long the two of them were in a heated discussion. At that point I intervened. Lonna was upset with me because I was not dealing with the situation and our child as promptly as she wanted. In fact, she accused me of standing up for the child.

Later, as we discussed the situation, it became clear that we were following patterns to which we had been exposed as children. Lonna reminded me that she rarely got away with anything in her family of origin. Everything she tried met with parental discovery. Still, she kept trying as an adolescent to get free of her parents' scrutiny. She can joke about it now, but at the time she was frustrated and determined to get away with something— anything. She was strong-willed and rebelled against her parents' expectations.

My parents rarely confronted me. They trusted me even when trust was not a wise position. I didn't rebel excessively, but I didn't need to because life went my way. Who knows what I would have done under tighter reins.

Lonna came from a "hands on" parenting style that was under-trusting and I came from a "hands off" parenting style that was over-trusting. In the incident with our child, we each acted out the parenting skills we had been taught without realizing where we had learned them. I accused her of being confrontational and suspicious, and she accused me of being too easy and naive. It was indeed fascinating to us once we realized what was happening. There we were as adult children and our childhood was still spilling over into our lives. There's a popular old saying, "You can take the boy out of the country, but you cannot take the country out of the boy." Similarly, we can say: *You can take the child out of the family, but you cannot take the family out of the child.*

Different Styles

On another occasion one wintery night in a Des Moines, Iowa restaurant, Lonna and I talked about our recent holiday visits to each of our parents' homes. Our son had broken something at my parents' home, which embarrassed and angered me. My parents said it was okay and that they would take care of it. But I was not sure it was okay because I had learned as a child that they did not always say exactly what they were thinking. They might excuse a misbehavior just to avoid a scene. In my mind they were being too easy on my son just as they had been too easy on me.

But did I say anything about my thoughts and feelings? Of course not! I did the same thing they did. We all avoided a conversation that might have been unpleasant. This was my *protecting* family personality at work.

Next, Lonna and I reviewed our visit with her parents. While there our children exhibited some of their sibling rivalry—a drain on parents but a reality in most homes. Lonna's parents told her that she should be able to manage the children better. Immediately she rebelled against her parents' expectations, and in no time the three of them were in a heated discussion. They had little trouble conveying their thoughts. Lonna did not think they were being fair, and they did not think she was being respectful. We were seeing Lonna's *ruling* family personality in action.

As we sipped our coffee, Lonna asked for my opinion about her relationship with her parents. The confrontations bothered her. She knew she was just as much to blame as they were. As deeply as the three of them (Lonna is an only child) cared for one another, Lonna struggled with feelings of being on trial before her parents. And she wondered if that would ever change.

I reminded her of the efforts her parents had made for her as a child, like the majorette uniforms her mother had sewn, her dad's coaching that helped her beat the top math student in her class, and many others. Both parents believed in her, which instilled Lonna with a high level of confidence. "I know there are a few things about your parents that really bug you," I said. "If you expect them to see the light or change, then you are going to be disappointed. They will never act the way you want them to act. Don't hang your hope on their change of behavior." Tears began to trickle down my wife's face.

"Lonna," I continued, "your parents are not perfect and it is unfair and unrealistic for you to expect perfection of them. Even the best families have some difficulties. Do you think it is possible for you to accept them just as they are? Do you believe it would help you enjoy them even more than you already do?" I told her that acceptance would not terminate difficult encounters. The issue was not to let these incidents spoil the many good experiences they had enjoyed together.

After talking about Lonna's parents, it was her turn to confront me about my parents. "Dave, I know you hardly ever disagree with your parents about anything," she said. "But I know there are things that bother you about them."

"You're right," I agreed. "Probably they were too protective and made life a little too easy for me. This sounds crazy, but I wish they would not have let me quit football my sophomore year in high school. They did not make me follow through on my commitments. I have no doubt that they loved me. But they gave in too quickly. I wonder if part of it had to do with my accident in the sixth grade when I lost vision in one eye. Maybe they felt sorry for me. I know it hurt them."

The conversation that night was a catharsis for both of us. We arrived at a point in our relationships with our parents that allowed us to love them more than we previously had. We could look beyond the minor mistakes and admit to one another that we were glad to have the parents we had; the positives far outweighed the negatives. We hoped that our children would do the same for us in the future.

Those talks about our families of origin have helped Lonna and me understand one another. Our marriage has benefited and so has our parenting. We are very similar to many of our friends. Almost all of us, as adult children, have issues to deal with in regard to our parents. It is not an indictment against parents, but a recognition that all families are in the process of learning how to live with each other—whether in the same home or separated by many miles.

As an adult child you may feel hopeless or disillusioned about your family of origin. My goal is to help you understand your family past and break some of the crusty barriers that have separated you from your parents. Don't yield to the temptation to ignore your problems. If you do, you are letting the past control you or overly influence your future. As an adult child, deciding not to do anything or deciding not to decide are decisions in the wrong direction. You may not be able to contact your parents directly, but at least you can discover the personality of your family of origin and thus understand yourself better.

Family Structure

Before we explore family personalities, we need to take a look at family structure. Families are dynamic, not static. They are constantly changing. What you see today will be different six months from now. However, even though there is constant change, most members of a family fall into a habitual pattern of relating to each other. Most kids can pretty well tell you what their parents will say if they bring home bad grades. Wives know how husbands will react in certain situations, and vice versa. Sometimes our family members are so predictable that we don't even listen to them because we know exactly what they are going to say.

We're talking about what I term family interactional patterns. These patterns are the basis for the structure of every family. Every family has a structure, though some structures may be more appealing than others.

The diagram on the next page shows the framework for depicting the functioning of a family. The outer circle encompasses the entire family system. The circle around the parents represents the parental subsystem. This circle includes husband and wife because both are responsible for parenting. Both parents are not always parenting at the same time. But supposedly both are in a cooperative effort to train and develop a good relationship with their children.

The circle around the children identifies the sibling subsystem. Obviously the children are not always coordinated with one another. But they exist in the same subsystem, just as the parents exist in their subsystem. Individually and corporately, children are under the authority and nurture of their parents. Children are separated from parents by the horizontal boundary which indicates a supposed difference between parents and kids. The circle around each person suggests that each individual is unique even though he/she is a member of the family system.

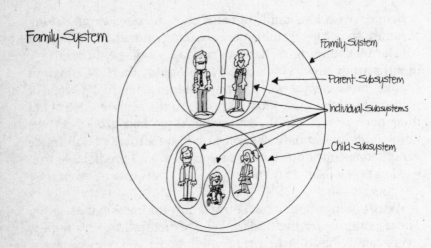

Parents are vested with authority in the family government and the marital subsystem is the foundation for healthy family functioning. There is definitely a direct correlation between a healthy marriage and a healthy family.

While the children are in the family system, it is the parents' responsibility to provide protection for their physical, emotional, and spiritual development. Mom and Dad are also charged with the job of equipping children to be responsible adults. There is no other social unit apart from the family system that can accomplish this task. Parents equip—or fail to equip—their kids without ever holding a formal class. Children develop a proper self-image, learn responsibility and spiritual values simply by being a part of the family system. Each family unit uniquely accommodates and adapts to the culture around it without compromising its values and traditions.

Family Goals

What are the goals of parenting? As the diagram shows, a child starts out under the protection of his parents. As the child matures, he is supposed to move toward the edge of the family system. At approximately age 13 he begins to experiment with being out on his own while his family operates as the training base. The ultimate goal of the parents is to allow and encourage the exit of the child. Hopefully, by the time of his exit, the child is sufficiently equipped to be a responsible adult.

Children have two fundamental needs which must be met in order to function effectively as adults—the needs for individuality and relationship. Another goal of parenting is to stimulate the balanced development of these two conditions.

Family Goal

Young Child   Adolescent Child   Adult Child

Individuality has to do with a sense of personal worth. A person with a healthy sense of individuality feels okay about being himself and likes who he is. He has an accurate view of his skills and limitations. He enjoys a high level of self-acceptance without needing to control others, and he does not want to be overly controlled by others.

Relationship has to do with the fact that there are other people in the world, and a person needs to communicate with and relate to others. A person with healthy relationship skills feels free to talk with others about his thoughts and feelings. He is not fearful or suspicious. He is sensitive to the feelings of other people and will act for the benefit of others, not just for himself.

Families vary in their accomplishment of instilling individuality and relationship in their children. The different family personalities described in this book reflect the different styles of parenting that tend to over-develop or under-develop these two areas. In other words, the balance of individuality and relationship in each person is heavily influenced by the personality of his or her family of origin.

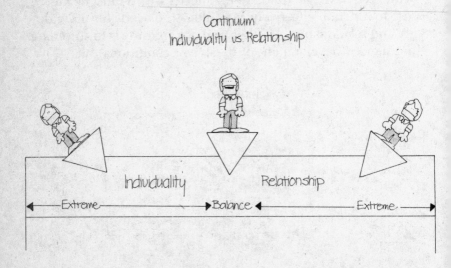

The continuum diagram shows two extremes: Individuality on one end and relationship on the other. The extreme of individuality pictures someone who is disconnected from relationships. He is self-centered and insensitive to others. He has little or no ability to establish and maintain healthy relationships. He is mean and harsh, and he acts out his emotions against others.

The person at the opposite extreme is dependent on people for acceptance. He has trouble discriminating between his own thoughts and feelings and those of his family. He is smothered by the family and generally indecisive and insecure. He feels warmth and protection, but it frequently suffocates his person-hood. He focuses on fitting in with the group, whereas the individualized person focuses on distancing himself from the group.

Most individuals do not live at one extreme or the other but somewhere in between. For example, a man may be somewhat insensitive and cynical, and perhaps a workaholic. His wife complains that he does not do a good job of communicating his feelings. He is probably overly individualized—somewhere between the extreme left and center on the continuum.

Someone who tends to depend on others for acceptance and opinions fits the relationship side of the continuum—between center and extreme right. He is bothered by situations where there is conflict. Sometimes he is unwilling to take risks or to pursue goals on his own. This person is under-developed in his individuality.

Family Personalities

There are five family personalities found along the contin-uum between individuality and relationship. You as an adult child should be able to identify the family personality that is most descriptive of your family of origin.

The Bonding Family: This family is a model of the balance between individuality and relationship. This family equips its children with a strong sense of identity and security and a capacity to relate to others. This family encourages its individual members to be all that they can be. They are not threatened by differentness.

The Ruling Family: This family has a tendency to be abrasive or insensitive in their relationships. The parents push their authority. Consequently the kids do not feel cared for, but they do know how to perform tasks.

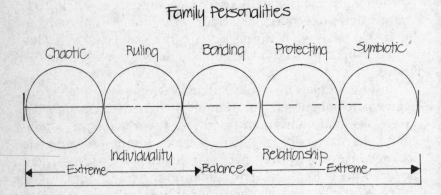

Family Personalities

The Protecting Family: Children in this family feel cared for, but often the parents do too much for them. Consequently the child is not allowed to develop a sense of personal confidence. The parents do not make him endure the consequences of his behavior.

The Chaotic Family: This family is disengaged from each other. Their knowledge of and interest in one another is limited. They are more like roommates than a family. Each individual looks out for number one. Caring for others is considered absurd or stupid. Children are neglected or abused.

The Symbiotic Family: Individuals in this family find it impossible to be self-directed because individuality is seen as a lack of allegiance to the family. They are weak as individuals but strong as a group. Children feel smothered in the family and guilty if they want to leave. Survival in the family comes from the ability to conform to the norms—drive the same kind of car, embrace the same political views, and like the same food.

Ingredients of the Family Personality

In the next five chapters, I would like to provide a profile of each of the five family personalities. In the process, we will explore how each family personality uniquely expresses the following seven ingredients:

1. Position on the continuum
2. Marriage relationship of the parents
3. Parenting style
4. Children's response to the family personality
5. Family dynamics—including communication skills, crisis management, and responses to the outside world
6. Religious influence and values
7. Exiting—how the children function as adults

As you read about each family personality you will probably discover one that best describes your childhood home. Knowing more about your family of origin will help you better understand why you feel and act the way you do as an adult child. You will recognize the affect of the family personality on your own development as a child. And, of course, who you are as a result of your childhood home has an effect on what you are passing down to your children.

As you review these family personalities, it would be wise for you to talk to someone about your perceptions. You may receive some good feedback from your spouse, a good friend, or a group. Lonna and I have been able to provide perspective for one another—to understand both the positives and negatives of our families of origin. If you are hesitant to talk with others, at least write your thoughts and feelings in a journal. I cannot overemphasize the importance of expressing your thoughts and insights about your family of origin in your own words. Use the framework of the next chapters to grasp and confront your family past.

The
Bonding Family

– 3 –

The Bonding Family

Katherine wasted no time getting to the point: "Edison, what are we going to do about those two boys of ours?" The couple had just been seated in the restaurant. They had decided to get away from the house to discuss the mounting tension between their two sons, Eddie and Howie. They weren't alarmed by the situation, but they did not want to see the boys' relationship deteriorate further. So they determined to put their heads together for some creative solutions.

Sixteen-year-old Eddie had always been a cooperative, fun-loving, pleasant kid. He rarely gave either parent any problems. Basically he was an easy child to be around and usually fit into any group. Eddie was not a leader, nor was he academically outstanding. But it didn't matter to Edison and Katherine. They were proud of their son. They believed that his character was a tremendous asset and they told him so.

Howie was a different story. He was a gifted child—very athletic, did well in school, and had many friends. Telephone calls for this 14-year-old were so common that no one else in the family bothered to answer the phone.

Edison and Katherine often remarked about the differences between the two boys. They were concerned about a breakdown in the relationship between the brothers. Recently Eddie had been irritable and quick to pick a fight with his younger brother. Then Katherine received a telephone call from school and learned that Eddie was on the verge of failing in two classes.

Edison and Katherine had always been sensitive to the fact that their older son was being followed by a multi-talented brother. They did not want Eddie's self-image to suffer because of Howie. Neither did they want to ignore Howie and some of his abilities just because they were concerned about how Eddie would handle the situation.

They decided to go home and have each boy write down what he thought his brother was feeling and why. The assignment was due in two days. Then the four of them would discuss the situation at a family meeting.

As they headed home, Edison reflected on how rewarding it was to be married to Katherine. He respected her insight into the boys because he wasn't always there with them. The couple was blessed with a good marriage and they worked hard to keep it together. They had their struggles, but they always worked them out.

They arrived home and Edison discovered that his parents, who lived in a distant city, had called while they were out. Edison returned the call and his dad answered. They talked about a project his dad was doing in the garage and about a couple of his friends who had just returned from a fishing trip. Then Edison's mother got on the phone and shared news about some of the other relatives back home. They laughed about a couple of situations involving some relatives who hadn't changed in years. Edison kidded his father just as he had done for the last 20 years.

Edison told his parents about the recent problems with Eddie and Howie. They listened with interest but didn't give much advice. Just before they closed their conversation, they talked over a few details about getting together in the fall.

As Edison put down the phone he thought about his youth. Things had not always been perfect with his parents, but generally speaking he could not complain. He respected his father, particularly for his integrity. He was a businessman who, as far as Edison knew, had never cheated anyone and had always provided very good service. Edison wished that they had done more things together when he was younger. Because of his dad's busy schedule, Edison thought he was closer to his mom. She was very attentive and inquisitive without being overbearing.

Edison never doubted that his parents loved one another. They weren't always expressive, but there was a certain charm about how the two of them related. They were pretty clear about who did what around the house and Edison could remember that he had his fair share of the chores.

Father and son had a few rough years as Edison was leaving high school and going into college. They did not see eye-to-eye about hair length back in the 1960s. Edison decided to try some pot while he was at college and he marched in a few anti-war protests. He never told his parents about the pot experimentation, but Dad found out about the marching and that did not go over well. But by the time Edison graduated from college the two of them had worked out their problems fairly well.

Edison took his first job and moved to another state. He and Katherine married soon afterwards, and they had the two boys and a girl. Edison had always enjoyed his parents' visits. They never invaded his life, but he knew that they could be very objective and helpful whenever he needed them.

At age 42, Edison appreciated his parents even more. They had been a model for him as he established his own family life. They had always supported him as a person and helped him discover some of his gifts and abilities as a kid. He intended to do the same thing with his children. And even when there were problems, such as the current situation with his two sons, Edison felt confident that they could be solved.

Definition

Edison came from a *Bonding family*. This family personality promotes a high level of individuality and proficiency in interpersonal relationship. In the diagram on the next page, we see that family members are connected to one another and yet, at the same time, distinct from one another. The parents work together and are in authority. The horizontal boundary demonstrates the structure—a difference between parents and children, but with flexibility and accessibility as shown by the openings in the boundary.

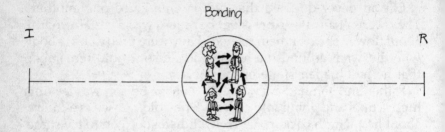

I

R

Bonding

In the Bonding family the parents are generally responsible and dependable. This family respects the rights and feelings of others and, at the same time, each individual respects himself as a person. Family members are encouraged to discover their talents and abilities. They also give to each other without feeling like they've been taken. The fact that each member is encouraged toward self-development shows a concern for one another's good—which is a picture of relationship. A parent who acts for the good of his child or spouse is a positive model to other family members. The example of Edison's parents provided a good model for their son, which he transferred to his own marriage and family.

Marriage Relationship

The parents show respect for one another through listening and cooperation. Success and accomplishment are acknowledged with positive responses from the spouse. Usually each parent is strong enough as an individual that jealousy, self-pity, and complaining are not routine. Husband and wife enjoy each other without too much distancing or smothering. They can afford to be apart because they are not overly dependent on one another. They spend time together as a married couple, giving priority to the marriage. Because of their solid relationship, this couple deals well with crises.

The Bonding couple's major contribution to the family is a solid foundation for their children. A strong marital coalition, good communication skills, and deep caring mix well, and kids appreciate it. The couple measures parenting success partly by results, but primarily by evaluating if they did the best they could do. They realize that their kids are individuals, and so these parents cannot totally control how their children will turn out as adults.

It is not absolutely necessary for a couple to get along well in order to produce a Bonding family. They may not agree in other areas, but they must collaborate as parents and lay aside their differences for the common good of their kids. Marital differences in the Bonding family rarely end in divorce. If a divorce does take place it is usually after the children have left the home and are established as adults.

Parenting Style

The parents work in coordination. One may serve as the lead parent, but he or she is backed up by the absent partner and the kids know it. When the kids test this union, they find out quickly, and sometimes painfully, that they cannot pit one parent against the other. This strong parental unit provides tremendous security for children.

Bonding family parents are students of their children—able to identify strengths and areas of needed development. Discussion about behavior and attitudes, plus planning for the future, occurs regularly. They keep in step with their children no matter what their ages are. They play with their children and discipline their children. The children are allowed space to be themselves, yet they also receive frequent hugs. The parents are proactive, not reactive. Proactive parents initiate training, loving, playing, and problem-solving before the children display their needs through misbehavior.

Parents maintain structure in the family. There are rules and expectations. In our diagram the children are not allowed to move above the horizontal boundary. Authority is maintained by Mom and Dad. As the children mature, the parents transfer increased responsibility for decision-making to their children, but parental authority in the family is never in question. Generally, parents won't allow any situation in which either parent becomes more affiliated with a child than with the partner.

If the children go against authority, discipline is usually swift. The child is not judged for being bad, but his actions are corrected for being disobedient. Mom and Dad are fairly effective in discipline because they do not need their children to like them or approve of them. The possibility that a child will be angry with his parents from being disciplined will not stop them if the child needs to be corrected. Bonding family parents love their children enough to endure temporary unpopularity.

Even though the structure of the Bonding family is solid, parents are not dictatorial. Children are free to disagree with parents as long as they are not disobedient or disrespectful. Children are encouraged to speak out. Parents will confer with their kids and involve them in the decision-making process more and more as they mature. These parents know that children learn how to run their own families by participating in the functioning of their childhood family.

Most children in the Bonding family feel like they have some influence over what happens in the family. They feel heard and respected. Almost everyone likes to choose things for himself, whether it is dessert or the color of a new sweater. Bonding parents allow for and encourage choices while reserving the option to overrule if the child's decision is inappropriate.

Bonding parents listen to their children and help them explore inward thoughts and feelings. If you grew up in a Bonding family you heard questions like, "Why are you feeling this way?" "What happened?" "Would you like to talk about it?" You were encouraged to talk about your inner thoughts, which helped you learn about the world of relationships. This action also helps the child define his own identity by clarifying what is inside him. It also assures the child that his feelings are acceptable.

Bonding parents tend to be verbally approving. There is little comparison between children, whether in or out of the family. Mom and Dad laugh with their children, hug them, and take pleasure in their successes. These parents realize their limitations and are wise enough to engage others in the training of their kids. For example, they may encourage contact with good teachers, coaches, and others who have skills that the parents do not have.

Children

Kids in the Bonding family feel secure, even though they may not realize it. They do not know the insecurity of a family breakup or poor parenting. Their parents have provided a consistent and stable environment. Children are protected from having to deal with adult issues over which they have no control and which negatively affect them.

When Bonding family kids do have problems in adolescence—such as involvement with drugs or rebellious attitudes—the difficulty tends to be short term. And their parents will rally around them—not smothering or attacking, but dealing with the behavior. These kids are nourished by their parents' confidence in them and strengthened when they join with them in overcoming the problem. The adolescent hears that his problem is temporary and it will be overcome.

Family Dynamics

When this family sits down together, they listen to one another. That is not to say that they never interrupt or fuss with one another. They do. However, Mom and Dad usually model and enforce hearing each other out. They are not compelled to change each other's opinions during discussions. Problems are confronted and attempts are made to resolve them.

Bonding family relationships are both static and dynamic. For example, Dad might regularly spend a lot of time with his teenage son, but he also takes his daughter out for a Coke occasionally to spend time together. This family experiences all the different relationships that exist in a family. On one issue Dad and Mom may agree, and on another issue Dad or Mom may side with one of the kids.

How does this family get along with the external world? Pretty well. Bonding family members are curious, interested, and usually involved. At the same time they have a sophisticated filtering system. They will not allow contradictory values and beliefs to permeate the family. Generally, they do not conform to anything which violates their values. They do not fear the external world's rejection. For example, Mom and Dad will listen as their children ask to do something which other kids are allowed to do. The parents thoughtfully consider the request. They are flexible and secure enough to change their minds or make an exception regarding a previous "no-no." However, if the request goes strongly against their beliefs or values, they will deny it. They will not hesitate to stand against the external world (other parents and kids) to uphold their values.

Religious Influence and Values

The Bonding family allows for differences of opinions and beliefs—up to a point. Make no mistake though: This family has a base of operations—a belief system to which they adhere. Their religious beliefs are beyond their own prejudices. For example, the family that holds the Bible as the source of truth and a guideline for values and moral behavior will attempt to live by these standards, not determine the standards. If a child says, "I don't believe in God," the parent does not say, "You must believe in God." Rather, the parent will inquire, "Tell me why you do not believe in God." The parent realizes he cannot make the child agree with him. So he lets the child explore. But in the meantime, just because Susie does not believe in God does not mean she is excused from family prayer time.

Assuredly, the Bonding family acts out its faith and values consistently. Children learn their beliefs as much by their parents' example as by their words.

Exiting

The parting of the child from the Bonding family is not usually traumatic or dramatic. Neither the parents nor the child are holding on or pushing away. The season arrives when parents and child alike sense it is time for the second birth—permanent departure from the home as an adult. Sadness and joy can both be present at this time. Bonding family parents let their children go without pushing them out early.

Kids exiting from Bonding families exhibit personal confidence and responsibility, and feel prepared for life. Parents continue to be active cheerleaders, but from a distance. Consultations with parents still occur, but parents are cautious not to give too much advice. When Bonding family kids choose marriage, they choose partners from the Bonding, Ruling or Protecting family personalities. Usually they do quite well in marriage and family life.

As adult children they find it a pleasure to return to their parents' home and a pleasure to leave. Being home with Mom and Dad is refreshing and fun. Leaving is easy because there is no discord or resurfacing of unresolved conflict. They are friends with their parents in addition to being their children.

The Bonding family is not a perfect family, for there are no perfect families. If your family of origin was a Bonding family, you likely have many pleasant memories, a respect for your parents, and few, if any, nagging problems with them. Count yourself fortunate and maintain the tradition.

The
Ruling Family

– 4 –
The Ruling Family

Sara would describe herself as an ambitious, loving person. She is driven to succeed and has done so throughout her 34 years. Sara has a master's degree in business and has moved quietly up the executive ladder in the corporate world. She credits much of her success to her parents' high expectations and the training she received from them as a child.

Lately Sara has suffered serious stomach problems and was diagnosed as having an ulcer. At work she experiences spells of dizziness and has lacked her usual flair. She falls asleep crying and awakes the next morning feeling more drowsy than when she went to bed.

Recently Sara was asked to mediate a dispute between her father and brother. She agreed because she felt obligated to do so. She also thought that if she could help out in this situation, she might receive a little more accommodation from her father and mother. Unfortunately the experience was like swimming into the jaws of hungry sharks. Sara felt disliked by both men, and the confrontation drained her even more.

Sara has never enjoyed a rewarding relationship with her father. Dad was the kind of man who always seemed to find fault with her actions. He was critical of any grade she received below an A. He persistently pushed her for performance. She never heard him say, "I love you, Sara." When she received her master's degree, he attended the ceremony and gave her a hug afterward. It was the closest Sara ever felt to her father.

Sara is disturbed because she's beginning to recognize how very much she is like her father. In the office she has a good reputation for getting the job done. However, under pressure she pushes her fellow workers and criticizes their poor performances. Secretly she feels superior to other employees because they do not work as hard as she does. A friend told her that she rubs people the wrong way. Those who work with her feel she is insensitive, overbearing, and picky.

Even though Sara hates to admit it, she knows that her friend is right. She never wanted to be like her father, yet in many ways she is his clone. She recognizes that she expects a lot from her fellow employees. She feels that if they are getting paid to do a job, then that job must come first, regardless of family commitments or outside involvements. As a result, she has few friends at work. Yes, people work with her, but they rarely socialize with her. So she feels isolated. Her irritability is at an all-time high and people are steering clear of her.

In the past, Sara just gritted her teeth and moved forward. She doesn't know how to admit defeat. But at this point in her life, given the situation with her father and her physical problems, Sara is beginning to wonder if she should reevaluate her life. The possibility that her troubles could be linked to her relationship with her dad makes her furious. She knows that he did her a favor in many respects because he pushed her as a child. But unfortunately he did not equip her to work with people. Sara feels most secure when she is performing at work, and she feels least secure in close relationships with other people.

Definition

As we can see from Sara's family of origin, the *Ruling family* is structured. It has strong and fairly clear expectations of its members. But the family's prevailing performance orientation compromises interpersonal relationships. A tendency toward criticism or fault-finding contributes to a lack of family closeness, often leaving individuals numb or resentful.

The Ruling family emphasizes rules over relationships. In fact, family members relate to each other through rules, chores, and tasks. They talk about tasks more easily than feelings. The ruling style exists because the family leader is incapable of, disinterested in, or unaware of interpersonal relationship skills.

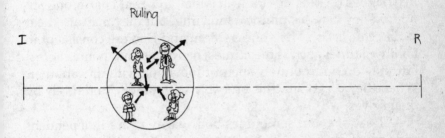

In the Ruling family diagram you see more space between family members than in the Bonding family. The horizontal boundary is less permeable, meaning that kids are strictly controlled and feel only mild personal interest from their parents. Typically one parent, usually the father, is in charge of the family and the marriage—a unilateral autocracy. One parent is boss and the other parent is assistant boss.

If you were a child in a Ruling family, you probably knew what was expected of you most of the time. You may not have heard many compliments, but you heard lots of directives. As an adult child from a Ruling family, you probably don't have a strong desire to spend much time with your parents. You have tried to be completely independent of them in order to escape their control. In close relationships you're uncomfortable discussing your feelings, and you may become irritated when others try to get too close. You may overreact to criticism by complaining or leaving.

Marriage Relationship

The partners in a Ruling family marriage are usually competent in their role assignments. Generally husband and wife have specific responsibilities, and one's love for his or her partner is proven by doing duties.

But there is an interpersonal vacuum in the Ruling family marriage. The kids do not hear Mom and Dad charm one another. They may see physical touching, but they may also hear verbal conflict and harshness. Mom and Dad are consistent in family routines such as mealtimes, bedtimes, and home chores, but they do not routinely spend time alone with one another. When they do go out, it is probably with others, and rarely by themselves.

At least one and sometimes both partners are independent and unwilling to be cooperative and self-sacrificing. Consequently the children see that their parents love each other conditionally. At home each parent has his or her chair, and rarely do they sit together. Even though they may feel warmth toward each other, they struggle with expressing it. Both of them are afraid of being hurt or taken advantage of, so they are defensive with one another.

Disagreements in Ruling family marriages are public. As a child in a Ruling family, you got tired of the arguments because they never seemed to solve anything. The fights were over the same issues most of the time. These marriages can get out of hand and end in divorce, especially for couples who chronically argue without reaching resolution. A hostile atmosphere produces a willingness to back out of the marriage commitment. Unfortunately a divorce does not necessarily terminate hostilities between the parents, and often the children remain trapped in the middle.

Parenting Style

The kids in a Ruling family feel like Dad and Mom have a book of rules and regulations, plus a never ending list of chores. Parental expectations are high and there is little margin for excuses or explanations. The Ruling family has a slight militaristic flavor, and if it was a corporation, the Ruling family could be accused of being sexist.

Often a child finds out he did something wrong after the fact. There is not always a lot of instruction; kids are just expected to know what to do and how to do it. For example, the son is chastised for mowing the grass "wrong," meaning he did not mow it the way Dad wanted. The problem is that Dad assumed his boy should know what he wanted. Dad is upset with his son. The son is upset because he did something wrong. Dad tells his son how he wants the job done in the future. Unfortunately Dad does not explore how his son feels about being rejected, nor does he apologize for not making his instructions clear the first time. As a result, the son learns to relate to his dad about tasks, but not about his inner thoughts and feelings. This is an example of how the family falls short in developing relationships.

The Ruling family "boss" can be quick to correct, displaying little patience. He will criticize without realizing he is critical. He forgets to look for the good points and offer compliments. He concentrates on how chores can be done better, which is often misinterpreted by his children as lack of acceptance. Enough is never enough.

Children

Children in the Ruling family relate to the parental boss more as a warden who is supreme and removed rather than as a caring, teaching parent. They get the impression that the parent is only interested in what the children can do for him, seeing only what they do wrong, not what they do right. Consequently they are pushed into open rebellion or cynical attitudes. They have trouble discussing a problem with their parents because they believe the parents will only find fault with them, not listen with an open mind. They expect another lecture, not a listening ear. They feel like their parents are not on their side but against them, so they emotionally withdraw.

Because the children are treated with insensitivity they learn to be insensitive toward others. They are independent because they are forced to be. Relying on self is more comfortable to them than relying on others. Some are very hard workers and do well in strict regimens. Others do not cooperate in school or other social settings because they don't like being told what to do. But in both cases their behavior is focused on rules, not relationships.

During adolescence these kids can give their parents fits. Teenagers often get into trouble by acting out against their parents. Some teens look for the love that is missing in the home by pursuing early sexual encounters, only to be further disappointed. They hear threats from their parents like: "If you do not straighten up, you'll have to leave." All in all, the teen years in the Ruling family can be full of conflict. The teens are taking vengeance for not being treated with more understanding and caring. When their ruling parent learns this, he typically responds: "What does he mean by 'no caring'? This kid has a lot more than I ever had—his own room, a car, plenty of food. He doesn't do near the amount of chores I had to do as a kid. What does he want?"

Often these kids are suspicious of people's motives, unable to take words at face value. They are not close to their brothers and sisters, except when siblings may be their only allies in the family. Thus siblings help them deal with the home atmosphere.

On the positive side, children in the Ruling family know that Mom and Dad will take care of their needs. Maybe kids would like more caring, but at least they have a fairly predictable and secure environment. Ruling families are proud of the fact that they do provide for their own.

Children in this family are familiar with work. They have confidence in their abilities to accomplish tasks, and many are driven to pursue lofty goals. Self-worth is usually directly related to accomplishments because that is what their parents recognize and reward. Billy learns that he can command Dad's attention by performing. When Billy hears, "Good job, Son," his job well done is his reward. Quite often he becomes addicted to performance, measuring his own self-worth, as well as the worth of others, on the basis of accomplishments.

Family Dynamics

Ruling family members have difficulty listening because they are more interested in making a point than hearing someone else's ideas. In dealing with issues, they are quick to tell you what they want and they attempt to get their way. Therefore it is difficult to talk through an issue. Compromise or giving in to another is a sign of weakness. The ruling parent feels he cannot allow his family members to see his weaknesses, fearing they will take advantage of him.

The family boss is rarely open to alternative opinions. He may say, "I don't care what you think about it, I have decided what I want done and how it will be done. That's the way it is, like it or not." As a result, some family members may keep information from the family leader in order to get their way. However, if he discovers their sneakiness he is even more difficult to work with. For example, Mom does not report to Dad their daughter's low math test score because Dad warned that a poor score would mean no prom. After the prom Dad inadvertently learns about the math test. He is upset, angry, and much more difficult to deal with on the next issue. This behavior provokes some kids to even more covert behavior.

The people who do best in Ruling families are those who do not tend to need or want a lot of warmth and attention. The task-oriented person does fairly well in this home. Sensitive people feel out of stride.

In regard to the external world, this family does not feel the need or even care about fitting into the environment—unless it's on their terms. They can appear arrogant, and sometimes they truly are. In committee meetings they are outspoken and not worried about whether others agree with them or not. At times they will coerce others, or at least make sure they are not coerced by others.

Normally joyous family outings, such as a picnic, can be trying and frustrating. Dad is upset with Tommy because the boy is not swinging the bat the way Dad told him to. He shows Tommy again, with the same results. Exasperated, Dad throws down the ball and bat and tells Tommy to go do it himself.

Mom feels sorry for Tommy, who is now in tears. Eventually they come back to the picnic table, but the conflict does not get processed. Dad feels like Tommy deserved the rebuke because he gave him plenty of chances. Mom feels like Dad is being too harsh, but if she objects to him she will be accused of taking Tommy's side. Tommy doesn't know what to do, but he feels like the whole thing is his fault.

Religious Influence and Values

Generally the parents in the Ruling family, or at least the overt leader, believe their values and persuasions are right. They are not open for debate, nor are they very willing to listen to other viewpoints. Unfortunately they may demand that their children adhere to their beliefs. As a result, children may carry out the form of their parents' religion but deny its power. They learn to perform for God in hopes of receiving His approval.

On the other hand, this family is to be admired because they persevere in their beliefs and values. They display strong religious allegiance and are consistent in their commitments. However, the children frequently reject the family belief system when they leave home.

Exiting

Children leave the Ruling family a little earlier than in the Bonding family. They want to get out and prove that they can do it on their own. When the child does leave, his departure is usually a relief for everyone. The child thinks, "I've had enough of my folks telling me what to do." Mom and Dad figure, "We've had enough of trying to raise this kid. It's time he learned how to make it on his own."

The adult children want their own space and are determined to take care of themselves. "I will make my own way," is their motto. Generally they will marry someone who is more relational, such as the adult child from a Bonding or Protecting family. After marriage, however, adult children of Ruling families may try to distance themselves from partners who want to relate on a more personal level.

For a few years after exiting, there might not be much contact between parents and adult children. Going home to see Mom and Dad is performed out of obligation. Adult children are braced for too much advice from the boss, especially when it is not requested. In many situations parents and offspring will get along well as long as they do not try to correct, convince, or control each other. When that occurs, there often is a confrontation. For example, as long as Granddad enjoys his grandchildren, everything is fine. But if he tries to tell his daughter how to discipline them, there could be a breakdown. She does not want to hear such advice unless she asks for it.

As the adult child from a Ruling family, you like having your way. You do tasks well. Even if you are down, you do not tend to quit—you know how to work. In relation to your parents, you likely have struggled with negative emotions—some so strong that you want revenge. You pay them back through lack of involvement and by keeping your distance. Be careful about treating your spouse and children in a similar fashion. The difficulties you encounter in interpersonal relationships as an adult are likely related to your Ruling family background.

The
Protecting Family

– 5 –
The Protecting Family

Tim and Ann have been married for 19 years. Tim is the oldest of three children. He was a very successful high school teacher, but last year he decided to shift to selling insurance. Ann is open to the change because she believes that Tim can be successful if he works hard. However, Tim's parents are quite concerned, especially his mother. Mom freely states her thoughts about how Tim should live even though he is 41 years old. She reminded Tim of all the time he had invested in teaching and the retirement benefits he would lose. If Tim had listened to her, as he has often done, he would not have made the career change. The issue disrupted their entire Christmas holiday. Tim knew that his mom was worried about him and the family. Every time his mother was upset with him, Tim wanted to escape. He did not want to upset her during the holidays, and he did not want to tell her to "bug off." He knew that if he did, Dad would be on his case too.

Tim was also upset with himself because he did not tell his parents that the new insurance job was his decision alone. He felt guilty for not pleasing them because they had always looked out for him. They paid the major portion of his college costs and bought him a car as a graduation gift. They helped Tim and Ann buy their first home, and Tim borrowed another large sum from them which the couple was still repaying. His parents had showered his three children with gifts and other opportunities he could not provide for them on a teacher's salary. He did feel grateful to them. However, their help created an uncomfortable sense of indebtedness within him. Mom and Dad always felt free to give their opinions. And they accused Tim of being unappreciative of them and all they had done for him and his family.

Whether he liked it or not, Tim knew that his parents' approval meant more to him than seemed appropriate for someone his age. And it really bugged Ann that Tim allowed his parents to persuade him what to do and what not to do, as had occurred many times in their married life.

For example, five years earlier Tim and Ann had made plans for a summer vacation. His parents called in March and announced that they would be traveling from their distant home to see them the middle of July—at the same time that Tim and Ann had planned their family vacation. Ann was upset because Tim allowed his parents to assume that the dates were okay instead of immediately informing them about the conflict. But Tim stewed for an entire month before he finally called his parents to break the news, causing a real furor. Ann believed that Tim's parents were upset with her because they assumed that she talked Tim into the vacation after her in-laws announced their plans to visit.

Most of the time Tim, Ann, and his parents got along well. But these sticky situations caused discord. When they occurred, Tim was upset for days and he found it hard to concentrate on work. He wished that he was stronger and not as sensitive to his parents' wishes. And by not expressing his true feelings, he knew he made the relationship more difficult for his parents, his wife, and himself.

Finally Tim decided to do something about the situation. He wrote a long letter to his parents in which he stated how he appreciated each of them and their efforts in raising him. He reminded them of specific events and situations which were meaningful to him. He admitted that he had let guilt and a sense of obligation overly influence his responses to them at times in the past. He told them he had been dishonest at times by agreeing with them when he didn't want to. He only agreed in order to avoid conflict and false guilt. He told them that he intended to take the new job. He asked them to support him in his decision even if it turned out to be a mistake.

Once Tim sent the letter he felt a lot better. He was more in control of himself, more comfortable with Ann, and he began to enjoy life more. He was no longer worried about trying to please people. He continued to be gracious, but now he was more straightforward.

Definition

Unlike the Ruling family which is more task-oriented, *Protecting family* members are very aware of each other's feelings. Disagreements are avoided because of a preference for a peaceful environment. To divert tension family members will forsake a controversial topic and talk about something else. Unfortunately they may not volunteer their true opinions and feelings. They compromise individuality because they fear tension or not being accepted. They feel insecure in disagreeable situations which do not bother most members of Ruling and Bonding families.

The Protecting family does a great job in the areas of family traditions and loyalty. Consciously focusing on the family is second nature to them. Children are very important and are often the center of attention, even to being the main determinant of the family calendar.

Note the movement of the parental coalition toward the children in the diagram. One or both parents have a priority commitment to their children which supersedes, or at least equals, their commitment to his/her spouse. There is less of a horizontal boundary between parents and children, which reduces parental authority. They still have authority, but they do not exercise it as much. The children soon learn that they have significant power and come to expect and/or demand attention and help. Family government is usually democratic, though sometimes heavily influenced by the children's vote.

Marriage Relationship

The marriage relationship in the Protecting family is basically stable, without a great deal of conflict. Each spouse seeks the other spouse's approval. Partners try to please each other and will sacrifice their own commitments, thoughts, and feelings to accommodate each other. Sometimes they give in to each other by choice and sometimes out of guilt or the need for acceptance. They do not like to hurt one another.

The major focus of the marriage is the children. With the arrival of children, Mom moves down into the sibling subsystem and her life becomes absorbed by the kids. She enjoys them as babies, but as they get older parenting becomes more stressful. The children are no longer as responsive to her nurturing, pampering, and protecting style. Occasionally she may reminisce about what it was like when they were young and manageable.

Sometimes one spouse resents feeling secondary to his children. In some marriages the highly protecting parent almost prefers that the other parent be less involved so the protecting spouse does not have to deal with a partner and the children. The attitude might be, "Just keep bringing home the paycheck so I can focus my attention on my children." Tension points are often ignored in this marriage because one or both partners do not communicate well. Sometimes it is easier for husband and wife to talk to their friends about their problems than to talk to one another.

Being involved in activities as a couple is rare because they do not like to leave the children. Consequently the marriage may suffer from lack of closeness. It is as if the marriage reaches a plateau during the active parenting years. When the children leave the home, the couple often has to renegotiate the marriage relationship.

Parenting

Children in the Protecting family receive loads of attention and support. Parents provide broad guidelines for activity. They are not permissive in the sense of letting the kids do everything they want to do. But parents will back off from a rule if a kid offers too much resistance. These children do not feel discouraged by a "no" response because they have learned that Mom and Dad often give in. Parents are so concerned about having a good relationship with their children that they will do almost anything to keep their children from being upset with them. It is almost as if the parents need consent from the children to parent.

Sometimes it goes so far as the parent asking the child what he wants and then accommodating the child. For example, Dad and Mom tell Lori, their junior high daughter, that she can go to a Friday night movie with her friends. Lori tells them that the gang is going out for pizza after the movie and one of the other parents will bring her home by 11:00 P.M. The parents resist the pizza part because Lori has a Saturday morning cheerleaders' practice. Lori throws a fit and accuses them of taking away all her fun. After a few tense moments Mom or Dad or both give in and tell her it will be okay this time. Now everybody is happy.

Thus the parenting style settles into a giving mode. Wanting their children to have all the advantages, parents enroll them in lessons, buy them all the popular toys, treat them to special events, and may even do some of their schoolwork for them.

When the child has a problem, the parents do everything they can to help him out—and sometimes bail him out. Unfortunately Protecting parents often over-protect their children from the consequences of wrong or inappropriate behavior. Parents rescue because they care, but the caring sometimes goes overboard. This action reinforces the child's self-centeredness and hinders the development of personal character. He does not learn how to persevere in difficult circumstances. Children subconsciously surmise that they deserve to have life go their way. Later on as adult children they often try to find peer-parents—such as a spouse or friends—to take care of them or bail them out of trouble. If no help is available, they may run from problem situations.

Occasionally Protecting parents are too protective. They will not let a child make decisions, or they prohibit a child from playing sports for fear of injury. They ride him constantly about his schoolwork because they do not want his teacher to think they are bad parents. The kids learn to fear not fitting in. The parents are influenced by what other adults think of them. Sometimes Mom and Dad communicate an anxiety about life and, as a result, the adult child searches for security. The net effect of over-protection is that it discourages individuality.

Because the parents cherish a warm family atmosphere they tend not to be demanding. They do not push and command like Ruling parents. A disciplinary statement might be, "I wish you wouldn't do that," whereas the Ruling parent would say, "Don't do that anymore, and if you do, this will be the consequence." Diplomacy is the preferred method of parenting, with infrequent or no corporal discipline. Sometimes parents use guilt to get results: "After all the things I've done for you today, the least you could do is clean up the dishes like I asked and not complain about it." Parents threaten more than they follow through.

Protecting parents could be accused of being naive about their children. They may think that their kids would never do what some other kids do. The children have a lot to say about what happens in the family. In a single parent Protecting family, the children may be more in control than the parent.

Children

If you grew up in a Protecting home, your parents were always looking out for you. You knew they loved you and believed in you. They played with you, cuddled you, and smiled approvingly at you. You knew your parents were devoted to you; it was almost as if they were your slaves. Almost every whim was satisfied. And you probably got used to it; it felt good.

Children from a Protecting family are usually well-trained socially. They show respect and they conform in social and school situations. These kids are capable of openness and strong interpersonal relationships.

However, as teenagers they easily fall prey to peer pressure. Since they have always been accepted by their parents, they may not know how to deal with lack of acceptance in a peer group. Consequently peer acceptance is extremely important. They want and need to fit in because group rejection is too painful. Their sense of worth comes from peer acceptance, so they accommodate themselves to the group's status quo. If a teenager does not have the "in" clothes, hairdo, or status-gaining possessions, he will pressure his parents to provide them for him. He will end up at odds with his parents if Mom and Dad show any resistance to his participation in the peer group.

In order to get his way, the Protecting family teenager will accuse his parents of not caring for him. He often manipulates them with arguments to do what he wants. He does to them what they did to him at an earlier age—uses guilt and self-pity to get his way. The result is a hostile-dependent relationship with Mom and Dad. He does not want them to tell him what he can do, or to overload him with chores. But if he needs ten bucks or a ride he feels free to ask.

This teenager is not secure enough to risk being spurned by

the group, and he may compromise himself to maintain membership. When he was younger his parents were his security. When there was a problem they protected him and he depended upon them. Now the teen's peer group can replace the parents as the primary source of his security. However, this means that the parental goal of balance between individuality and relationship is not met. The teenager has not learned to be secure enough with himself to stand alone when necessary.

Family Dynamics

Protecting family members communicate with sensitivity and respect for one another. But their effectiveness is compromised by a tendency to avoid uncomfortable situations and/or cover their real needs with superficial complaints. For example, someone may accuse, "You never take me to a movie!" instead of asking, "Will you please take me to a movie?" One family member will behave as if there is no problem with another, then complain about that person to a third family member. Amazingly they often know what others in the family are thinking and feeling. They are really tuned in to one another. There is a lot of "communication" taking place in the Protecting family even when no words are uttered.

In a crisis these family members demonstrate a tremendous amount of support and protection for one another. When one suffers an accident the others feel sorry for the victim. But while they rate high in caring, they are not as effective in decision-making. They spend too much time asking each other about the best action to take. In wanting to make the right decision, procrastination sets in.

In dealing with the outside world, Protecting families seek to fit into the status quo. It is their way of maintaining acceptance and security. External opinion may be a more powerful agent of personal security for them than their own judgments. Since the confidence of Protecting family members is underdeveloped, they fall prey to the judgments of others whom they unwittingly empower to dictate their worth and sense of security. Consequently they are constantly figuring out how they can fit into the group norm.

They are suspicious of, and sometimes threatened by, those who are different. They may be very dependent upon trusted authorities to tell them what to believe and do. For example, if someone they trust has convinced them that unions are bad, then they will not be comfortable around someone who is a union member, especially if that person is trying to recruit them. Because they lack personal confidence and strength, they rely on others to tell them what to think and how to act.

Religious Influence and Values

Protecting families are very loyal to their beliefs and churches. They fit in well at church and are not generally disruptive. However, they may tend toward legalism. Their insecurities may lead them to adopt outward spiritual behaviors to reassure them of their inward faith. They feel threatened by people who have different theologies or forms of worship.

Exiting

Whereas exiting the Ruling family takes place prematurely, Protecting families delay the second birth of their offspring. Parents struggle with letting the kids go. The kids are willing to leave physically, but still may expect financial support, advice, or help from Mom and Dad when they need it. They are used to having things go their way and being rescued when they don't. When faced with difficulty, they rely on Mom and Dad to assist them.

In a sense the adult child from a Protecting family is only pseudo-independent. As the diagram on the next page illustrates, instead of the child exiting the family, the family circle often expands to delay or prevent the adult child's escape. The result is an ever-expanding family circle. In some senses the adult child may not want to escape. In leaving the family of origin, some adult children experience guilt-feelings or anxiety because they have abandoned their caring, protective parents. They worry about how to care for themselves without their parents' help.

Space Expanding

Usually the adult child will marry someone who is more decisive and less controlled by the external world than himself. Then, even though adult children like the security of a marriage, they may be bothered by the lack of sensitivity in their spouses. They may feel victimized by their partners who always seem to get their way. But the adult children of Protecting families choose their victim role because of insecurity and/or a need for acceptance.

Most adult children remain actively involved with, and loyal to, their parents. They enjoy going home and they feel secure being there. When they visit it is easy for them to fall back into the child's role of being attended to by Mom and Dad. If the adult child's spouse is not cooperative with the Protecting family's need to be together and maintain traditions, he or she may become quite unpopular.

It's not unusual for Protecting parents to sabotage an adult child's marriage, for in their minds the family of origin takes priority. Despite that possibility, most of the time the adult child has a workable marriage. In addition, he is loyal to his family heritage, seeks to maintain the family legacy, and has active contact with the family of origin.

As an adult child from a Protecting family you may have some conflicting emotions. You appreciate your parents' love and interest, but may also feel angry with them for making life too easy for you. You have been hindered as an adult because Mom and Dad did not make you solve some of your own problems and face the consequences of your actions. They cared too much. So when you are with them you may vacillate between appreciation and anger.

You may also struggle with the habit of expecting others to serve you. Your parents gave in to your needs, and you got the idea that your needs were more important than others' needs. You may expect life to go your way. As a child you received what you wanted. You pleaded, pouted, or threw tantrums until you got your way. You may have become addicted to your own importance, depending on others to meet your needs.

You may find yourself being a mediator between your parents and your spouse. You'd like to satisfy both so everyone will get along. However, a choice is often necessary. You may not be able to please both sides. So you must decide that your first loyalty is to your spouse, not to your family of origin.

As an adult child one of your biggest challenges is to give up depending upon others—parents, spouse, friends, the government. Get out of the trap of needing to fit in and to be liked. Accept the fear of rejection as real, but realize that the fear is a bluff. Rejection from others is not nearly as harmful as being controlled by your fears. You have inherited from your family of origin the quality of relating. Now comes the opportunity to develop your individuality. Fortunately this is easier for most adults than developing relationship skills.

The
Chaotic Family

– 6 –

The Chaotic Family

Bill came to me for counseling because his marriage was on the rocks. After a 19-year parade of hurtful episodes, his wife Lucy decided she was fed up.

Their problems came to a head one night when Bill arrived home from work. Their 16-year-old son Todd was watching TV. Bill asked Todd if his homework was done, but Todd didn't answer. Bill asked again, and when Todd failed to respond Bill lost control. He jerked Todd up by the shirt and yelled, "I asked you a question and I expect an answer!" Lucy came into the room and tried to separate them. Bill pushed her out of the way and went after Todd. When it was over, Lucy was in tears and Bill had left the house.

Bill was always having confrontations. He was tough to get along with at work, but his employer kept him around because he was such a great salesman. He intimidated people into buying from him and he made plenty of money. It did not bother Bill that he intimidated others at work; in fact he liked the feeling of power. But at home it was a different story. He swore he would never hurt his kids like his dad had hurt him. Bill asked me, "How come I am so mean to the people I love? When I get into a family fight I feel like I must win."

Bill finally agreed that he needed to work on his problem. We started by talking about Bill's life history. His childhood home was a sham. He had two older sisters, two older brothers, and one younger sister. Dad was gone most of the time, but when he was home, Dad and Mom frequently fought. Bill felt sorry for his mom because she tried her best to please Dad, but with little result. She took the children to church when Bill was young, but they were forever getting into trouble in Sunday school. Bill and his siblings would take on the other kids and beat up on them. As a result, Bill's mom did not feel welcome at the church and they all stopped attending.

Mom had to work, sometimes leaving early in the morning and not returning home until late afternoon. In the summer the kids fended for themselves. Lunch consisted of crackers, cheese, cold soup, and on a good day, hot dogs. The children lacked adult supervision, and it seemed like Bill's older brothers beat up on him all the time. Once the boys pulled out Dad's shotgun and loaded it. It went off and blew a big hole in the ceiling.

Bill hated his dad, and his brothers and sisters felt the same. Dad would tease Bill about being weak and then punch him in the shoulder. Bill couldn't wait to grow up and escape his Dad's abuse. "Then I'll bust him and let him feel the pain," Bill told himself.

When Bill was 12 years old, his oldest brother died in a motorcycle accident. The loss was a tremendous shock to Mom, but Bill's dad acted unaffected, which really bugged Bill. About a year later one of Bill's sisters was having school discipline problems and his other brother was placed on probation for selling beer to minors. A social worker came by to talk to the kids. When Dad found out about it he was enraged. He told his family never to talk to the social worker again.

As far back as Bill could remember his dad was a miserable and mean person. He had a bad temper. When he was upset with the kids he would threaten to send them to a foster home. Then he would tell them about his experiences in a foster home— how he was beaten repeatedly and worked unfairly.

High school was a joke for Bill. He disliked school except for metal shop where he could work on cars. He loved to play practical jokes at school, but they were mean jokes. He only stayed in school to play football. He loved to hit people, and in football hitting was legal. It gave him a sense of power to cut down a blocker and tackle the ballcarrier.

By the time he was 16, Bill's parents only communicated when they were fighting. The family was like a human buzz saw—ripping up the members that were left. Even though he did not like school, Bill preferred it to being at home.

After high school, Bill joined the Army in order to get far away from his dad. He left the family to follow three rules: People are pawns to be used for one's own convenience; feelings are a sign of weakness; and trusting others is stupid. He never returned home except for his mother's funeral.

While in the military Bill met Lucy. After a wild courtship, Lucy's pregnancy brought the couple to marriage.

Definition

Bill came from a *Chaotic family*. The Chaotic family is poorly organized and in a constant state of ambivalence. It tends to be conflictive, problem-plagued, and insensitive to the children's needs. Children are ignored or abused, with a lack of relationship between them and their parents.

The Chaotic family is always flying apart. They live in the same house, but the environment is neither fun nor safe physically, emotionally, or spiritually. The horizontal boundary is fixed and rigid, allowing no permeation between parents and kids. In addition, there is frequently a vertical boundary separating the spouses. Family members are not close, and if one member is going to survive, he must do so without the assistance of the other family members.

The Chaotic family is at the extreme left end of the individuality-relationship continuum, unable to relate well with others. Chaotic families can be identified by the great distance between family members, the lack of marital coalition, and the emotional abandonment of children. Chaotic families are not unique to any socioeconomic group. In a wealthy family a nanny may be assigned the task of parenting while the parents relate to their children only formally. Children relate to their parents as acquaintances, demonstrating little affection.

Marriage

The marriage in a Chaotic family is a non-marriage. The couple may have procreated children, but there is little or no love between husband and wife. They spend no energy nurturing the marriage. They fight regularly, and occasionally war breaks out. Separations and threats of divorce are common. In fact, many of these marriages do end in divorce.

In some Chaotic families, the parents get along pretty well but they abandon their children emotionally or physically. Because of limited marital coalition and very poor parenting, the Chaotic family may attract help from their extended family, the church, or the community at large.

Parenting

In the Chaotic family there is great abuse to relationships. The parents stir up anger in one another and there is little relationship between the parents and the children. Parenting is inconsistent—sometimes depending on the moods or life-style of the parents. Some children are worked like slaves while others are left to their own devices. These parents are irresponsible—either abandoning their children emotionally and physically, or treating them harshly.

Mom and Dad spend their time doing what they want to do. The kids are not sung to at night, hugged very often, or cared for when they are hurt physically or emotionally. When they get out of line they are usually over-disciplined. Verbal taunting, teasing, and faultfinding burrow into the tender souls of the children. These parents control their children through intimidation, threats, and power. Discipline is erratic, harsh, unfair, and sometimes unbearable. Frequently discipline focuses on putting the kid down instead of correcting his behavior.

Children

Children in the Chaotic family feel threatened and unloved. Much of the time they are angry or depressed. In a sense the family situation is so unpredictable that children are unaware of feelings. They simply exist from day to day in a tense and stressful family atmosphere.

These kids get the impression that they are unwanted in the family—an imposition on their parents' money and time. They sense that their parents wish they weren't around, or they decide that their parents would be better off without them. For sure, children get the message that they are not welcome in the home past high school, if that long. Sometimes a child concludes that he must be very bad because no other parents he knows treat their children the way his parents treat him. He may want to leave or to die. However, the predominant feelings of most kids in Chaotic families are revenge, anger, and bitterness.

Anything these kids know about positive family life is learned through their friends' families. Mom and Dad provide little or no training and guidance. The children who survive best are those who can teach themselves or who are lucky enough to find a mentor outside the family.

Adolescents from Chaotic families are hardly ever naive or innocent. They are forced to grow up quickly and are more worldly-wise than their counterparts from other families. Their spending money and possessions must come from their own efforts.

In school they are unruly and they earn poor grades. Social taboos like smoking, drinking, and promiscuity are experienced early. Kids are quick to resist, insult, and confront authority. They are beginning to ignore and abuse society as they have been ignored and abused in their families. There are no rules at home, so they roam freely—except when a parent gains temporary control through a physical beating.

Family Dynamics

In a sense it is contradictory to speak of Chaotic family dynamics because there is no family per se. There are individuals residing within the four walls that most people call a home. But this home is merely a stopping-off place for these people. Family members may not see each other for days on end, which is fine with them. The kids avoid bringing their friends home because of the unpredictability of their parents. They have been embarrassed before and they do not want to risk it again. They do not go on outings or vacations together. If you grew up in a Chaotic family you are hard-pressed to identify any family traditions or remember many pleasant times from your childhood.

The Chaotic family does not keep in step with the external world. They live in distrust of others and are generally unwilling to cooperate. They abide by rules only when it is convenient for them, not because these rules are good for society.

Religious Influence and Values

Not many Chaotic families have a strong spiritual orientation. If they do, the belief system may be somewhat intact, but the practice of compassion is limited. They tend to be attracted to dogma on power and control. They like confrontation, but are unwilling to practice patience and perseverance with others. They hold that their beliefs are right and everyone else's are wrong.

In a Christian Chaotic family, the kids usually rebel against the parents and their faith. These families may use the Bible as a weapon. For example, a child may be spanked unmercifully for disrespect with the parent justifying his actions by his interpretation of the Bible.

In most Chaotic families, religion is considered wimpy and weak. To them it is absurd to be concerned about heaven when they are worrying about how to survive today. If an adolescent in the family turns to God, he will likely suffer sarcasm, chiding, and rejection from his family: "Who do you think you are? We know what you are really like. Don't give us this God stuff." If the adolescent reacts negatively to these insults, he will only confirm his family's claims that he has not changed.

Exiting

Kids usually leave the Chaotic family prematurely with unresolved conflicts and a general distaste for the family. Sometimes they go so far as to become pregnant, commit a crime, get placed in a foster home, or join the military to get out of the home. There may be some contact with a parent after departure, but little active involvement. Exiting children do not carry a positive feeling for other family members. Sibling contact is rare because they feel no need or desire for such contact.

When adult children from Chaotic families marry, they usually have problems relating to their spouses and children. They are very self-oriented, they do not trust others, and they don't know how to relate. Even though they may want to be good spouses and parents, they have no positive family of origin model to follow. So when they are frustrated with family members they resort to attacking, which only widens the separation. Work situations are the same. They are abrasive and they make others uncomfortable.

As an adult child of a Chaotic family, your major challenge is to admit to yourself and to a few trusted loved ones that you need to learn how to relate to other people. That admission is difficult. You tend not to trust others. You must risk being vulnerable and discover that you don't always need to be in control.

Over the years you may have realized that you are a person without a conscience. You have physically and emotionally inflicted pain on others without remorse or regret. You likely have a bad temper or a get-even mentality. Adult children of Chaotic families are capable of violence. This condition needs attention.

You must spend some time reviewing your past and dealing with your parents. They are likely an integral part of your personal struggles. The effort to resolve the past requires more than just forgiving your parents. It also means gaining freedom from your family of origin so that it no longer controls you. It is an assignment worth undertaking. There will be some suggestions in later chapters to help you do this. But you may also need further help from a friend or professional counselor. Don't hesitate to seek that help. It may be the only way you can save your marriage and family.

The
Symbiotic Family

– 7 –

The Symbiotic Family

Diane, a 35-year-old mother of two pre-adolescent boys, was in my office talking about her depression. "Ever since childhood I've felt overwhelmed by my mother. It's like she gets inside of my mind. When I tried to stand up for myself as a teenager, she had this uncanny ability to make me back off. I'd walk away feeling horrible, thinking I did something wrong. Even now when I talk to her on the phone I feel like she can control me."

Diane's description is a classic case of the adult child from a Symbiotic family. When I first met her, Diane could not remember a time in her life when she had not felt down. She moved slowly. Her thinking was impaired. Simple decisions, such as whether to buy one or two gallons of milk, were a challenge. She struggled through each day and welcomed the night as temporary relief.

She talked about her husband, Frank, and mentioned his patience with her. She was amazed because nothing bothered him. He made decisions quickly and was very direct. But she disliked his job because it had forced them to move. On the positive side, the recent move had created some space between Diane and her parents. Frank had a few disagreements with Diane's parents, which made her very uncomfortable. She could not believe that he was not intimidated by them. Diane felt more secure with Frank than with her parents.

It soon became apparent that Diane's depression was a function of her underdeveloped self. All the pieces were there, but they had not been put together. Her parents were so busy using her to meet their own needs that she had been shortchanged.

81

Diane could not understand how her parents ever got to-gether. There was very limited affection. Mom ran the family, including Dad. Her tools were complaints, self-pity, and accusa-tions. Mom disliked Dad's community activities, but he never backed off from them. When Diane was younger her dad's mother lived with them. Diane's mom still complains about it. Mom and Grandmother never got along, and to hear Mom tell the story, Diane's grandmother pampered her son. Diane's mom thought that her husband never really grew up.

Diane could not figure out her mother. At times she seemed so strong, controlled, and independent. On other occasions she acted as if the entire world was against her. Mom was sure Diane liked Dad more than her. She would ask Diane, "Do you love your father?" But before Diane could answer she would say, "Of course you love your father. You probably love him more than me. It's not fair because I'm the one who must discipline you."

Mom tried to run every area of Diane's life. For example, when they went to a restaurant for lunch, Mom would answer for her when the waitress asked for their orders. Diane just sat there and smiled politely at the waitress. She hesitated to tell her mother that she did not like what had been ordered for her. If she did, Mom would accuse her of not being appreciative.

Diane felt very insecure around her mother. She was con-stantly trying to figure out what to say or do that would keep their relationship peaceful.

Diane made progress during counseling as she began to understand her family of origin. Consequently she tried to be more decisive in her choices. She told her husband things she would normally keep to herself, and she started to detach her-self emotionally from her family of origin. As she did, her depression began to lift. Seeing Diane transform was like seeing a mannequin coming to life.

One day during a counseling session, Diane announced that her parents were coming for a visit. They had called to inform her when to pick them up at the airport. She was so surprised that she wrote down the information and agreed to their instructions. I noticed a definite change in Diane's attitude. She told me that she did not feel prepared to deal with them and feared that her progress from counseling would be compromised. Also she was afraid that her parents would affect her boys like she had been affected.

Diane's visit with her parents was both successful and unsuccessful. Through much preparation and forethought she initiated the planning of activities without seeking her parents' advice. She deflected her mother's attempts to speak negatively about her father. When she felt guilty or anxious, Diane told herself that the uneasiness would eventually leave.

There was one incident in which her parents started talking to the boys in the same manner that Diane had been talked to as a child. Instinctively Diane grabbed her children and took them to their rooms. She was so disturbed that she hyperventilated. Hearing the words her parents directed toward the children prompted a flood of frantic feelings from the past. She had to remind herself that this was her home and that she was in control. After settling down, Diane returned to the living room and talked calmly with her parents.

Diane is still dealing with the affects of her Symbiotic family of origin. But she is making progress. She realizes that the problems she endured as a child do not need to be transferred to her children.

Definition

The *Symbiotic family* is characterized by a strong family orientation, with attention focused almost exclusively on the children. These families overdose on relationship, usually because one or both parents are severely obsessed with attachment to the children in the face of a fragile marriage.

The Symbiotic family resides at the extreme right end of the individuality-relationship continuum. Notice in the diagram on the next page how the family members are huddled together, making it difficult to tell them apart. There is no horizontal boundary between parents and children, meaning that the parents have abandoned the marriage as a foundation for the family. The parents invade the boundary of each child, attempting to create clones. Instead of encouraging each child to develop into a distinct individual, parents try to reproduce themselves in their children. Mom and Dad disallow individuality and foster dependency. At least one parent, and sometimes both, think and act for the child.

This condition can be termed abusive relationship. It is family closeness which is out of hand, gone wild. The parents ignore the child's individuality and crowd into his life. The parents are very committed to their children, but they are also very possessive. The dangers of this abusive relationship are quite subtle. How can anyone accuse a caring parent of doing harm to her child? But the damage is there, just as real as in the Chaotic family. The Chaotic family abuses the body; the Symbiotic family abuses the brain-psyche.

An adolescent in a Symbiotic family is kept in line by parents who make him feel bad every time he starts acting for himself. For example, a 14-year-old son does not enjoy summer camp because he feels bad about leaving his mother for a week. Before he left, she told him how much she was going to miss him. She confirmed her feelings with phone calls and letters to him at camp. He feels bad because Mom feels abandoned. So in order to avoid more bad feelings, he stays home next summer. He is so mentally attached to Mom that he is not free to do something for himself.

In the circle on the left, Mom is so much a part of her son it is difficult to tell them apart. He is so sensitized to her that he acts to please her at the expense of his own needs. The circle on the right shows an appropriate amount of space between the mother and son. This mother allows and encourages her son's individuality.

Marriage

In most cases the Symbiotic marriage is unhappy, but not outwardly. This couple is cordial with each other and they cooperate in social functions. Marriage is part of the social standard which they feel compelled to meet. In some of these marriages you find an emasculated husband controlled by a domineering wife who constantly complains about his weaknesses. In counseling she may express deep hurt because of her husband's inattentiveness, but when he tries to console her she rebuffs him. He cannot please her either way, and that is the source of her power.

The Symbiotic couple looks happily married. But there is little romance or genuine caring because one or both partners sabotage it. Usually the one who fears abandonment moves toward the children because it is easier to control children than another adult. The marriage ends up under the influence of the partner who convinces the family of his/her exaggerated sense of weakness.

Parenting

Symbiotic parents are threatened persons who attach themselves to the children for security. Much of what they do for their children is really a function of meeting their own needs. The parental attachment begins before the child is able to discern the situation. A parent's actions are not usually premeditated, but they are addictive to both the parent and the children. The threatened parent is not usually passive, but outwardly independent and demanding.

How do Symbiotic parents control their children? One method is accusation. For example, parents ask, "Don't you want to give Mommy a kiss?" or say, "You are thinking of yourself again and not how it hurts Daddy." Another method is mind-reading. The parent constantly invades the child's mind. No private thoughts are allowed. The parent exposes the child's thinking by giving an interpretation to the child's tone of voice, body language, and facial expressions.

Another tool is guilt, which works wonders on children. Kids become so accustomed to guilt as a motivator that they carry it over into adult life. The "oughts" and "shoulds" work well, plus statements like, "Won't you feel guilty if you don't tell your mother what you are thinking?" For example, Dad repeatedly tells his daughter that she should not feel anger towards him. Whenever she feels anger towards him, she is afraid that he will read her mind. So she tries desperately to cover her feelings even more. Thus she is satisfying her dad's wishes and being a good girl. Unfortunately her individuality is impaired.

In order to gain acceptance from his parent, the child will try hard to adhere to what the parent expects. Mom says to her daughter, "Sally, bad things happen to little girls who have bad thoughts toward their mothers." So Sally does everything in her power to suppress or deny any bad thoughts towards her mother. The Bonding mother would accept Sally's bad thoughts as normal and help her talk about them. But the Symbiotic mother is crushed by a child's negativism and employs guilt or accusation to discipline Sally. In this way the Symbiotic parent maintains control.

Sometimes Symbiotic parents control their children by trapping them in no-win situations. For example, Mother comes home with two blouses for her daughter Kim. The girl skips to her bedroom to try them on. Kim happily comes out to model the blue one first and her mother responds, "Didn't you like the pink one?" If Kim says she likes the pink one, Mother says, "Then why didn't you try the pink one on first?"

But if Kim states that she doesn't like the pink one, she will be accused of being unappreciative. She is confused and frustrated, thinking she has done something wrong. Seemingly always caught in the middle and unable to please, the child will learn to forfeit her individuality by agreeing with the parent.

Children

Children in a Symbiotic family spend too much time attempting to figure out what the parent wants so they can conform to it. This inordinate focus on parental desires injures a child's individuality. Since the children do not like feeling bad, they try to anticipate what the parent wants and behave accordingly. As adult children they often employ the same methodology with their peers, employers, and spouses.

Adolescents from Symbiotic families are latent in social development. A Symbiotic 15-year-old may act like a 13-year-old from a Bonding or Ruling family. He is so used to figuring out what others want from him that he is a master chameleon. He wants to be told what to do and think. His peer group may take him away from his parents for some activities. But most of the time the parent maintains control by sabotaging his involvement with friends.

A teen in a Symbiotic family does not talk back to parents because he does not want to feel bad. He has many self-doubts and is tempted to back away from social contacts. Some even drift into deep psychological problems. Most Symbiotic adolescents suffer from some kind of emotional difficulty.

Family Dynamics

Most Symbiotic families operate routinely in their daily habits—regular meal times, social activities, summer vacations, and home chores. Home and family dominate their time. But an anxious atmosphere pervades the home, emanating from the parents and their insecurities. The adults are constantly concerned about fitting in at work, about whether their children are safe, or about how another family member will respond to something they say or do. The children pick up their parents' anxiety and they in turn become anxious.

Communication in the Symbiotic family is not conflictive. "Peace at any price" is their motto. Open conflict produces too much uneasiness. If there is conflict, it is from the hyper-sensitive adult who is quick to accuse or question when he or she feels threatened. Family members are so sensitive to each other that they have trouble conducting a productive conversation. They are more interested in being agreeable than in being honest.

The family is threatened by diversity. They are uncomfortable with any member who does not conform to family expectations. So an individual is not allowed to express his true feelings. For example, Mom asks Chuck if he wants a piece of pie. Chuck thinks to himself, "I really don't want any pie because I am full. But Mom might be offended if I say no." And if he answers no, Mom says, "Don't you like my pie, Chuck? I made it just for you." Chuck cannot express his personal preference without his mother being offended.

Group thinking is the order of the day in the Symbiotic family. Any member who does not adhere to the family traditions and beliefs is accused of being against the family. Symbiotic families distrust and dislike groups or individuals that are different from them. In order for an outsider to fit into the family, he must agree with the family. Areas of agreement might include child discipline, politics, education, or religious practices.

The Symbiotic family is caught in a bind in relation to the external world. On the one hand they want to be part of the status quo. They look for groups they can trust and give their loyalty to. On the other hand anyone who does not adhere to the Symbiotic family's loyalties is immediately suspect.

What are considered routine events for the Chaotic family create crisis for the Symbiotic family. A parent gone for a few days, a big fight between Mom and one of the kids, an injury that requires stitches—all are traumatic to the Symbiotic family.

Religious Influence and Values

If a Symbiotic family participates in religious activities they do so out of true interest. Sometimes they have a need to be told what to believe and how to practice it. These guidelines help them feel confident that they are doing what is right.

Occasionally God is a threat to them. They may have great fears about the loss of their salvation, or they may perform certain spiritual activities because they think God won't like them if they don't. Ironically the parents relate to God as their children relate to them—anxiously trying to please in order to be accepted.

Exiting

Children do not really exit from the Symbiotic family. They depart physically, but getting married and having children does not remove the adult child from the mental control of the Symbiotic parent. The emotional and mental programming is so strong that adult children from Symbiotic families of origin find it difficult to live independently.

Exiting is complicated because the parents keep expanding their circle of influence, absorbing their child's spouse and children. The adult child's parents may manipulate this closeness by giving gifts, extending loans, or questioning decisions. It is not uncommon for the adult child to feel trapped between his parents and his spouse. Symbiotic parents have been known to be quite upset with the spouse of their adult child when that spouse tries to pull the adult child closer to the marriage and away from the parents. Sometimes adult children seek out a strong partner who will help them escape Symbiotic parents.

Exiting is enhanced when a mentor helps an adult child discover and develop his individuality. The adult child needs help to discern where loyalty to family of origin ends and individuality begins.

If you are an adult child from a Symbiotic family, the best action you can take to honor your parents is to separate from them. Your parents likely will interpret your move as disloyalty. But don't let that stop you. Once you have collected your own thoughts and gained self-confidence, you will be able to love them legitimately, not from fear or obligation but from choice. Do not try to change them or make them understand. Reassure them that you care while you continue to separate. The family way is to grow up and *leave* your family of origin. Leaving does not mean cutting off the relationship, but it does mean standing on your own.

The Family Portrait

– 8 –

The Family Portrait

After reading about the various family personalities, you are probably reacting in one of two ways. Some of you identified your family of origin and recognized that some of your current marriage and family problems are the result of early programming from your parents. Now you want to know what to *do* about your problems. Others of you agree that this makes some sense, but you have a lot of questions. Perhaps you find it hard to identify your family of origin because your family situation was so traumatic. Or maybe you're confused because at various times you lived in families with different personalities—the result of adoption, foster care, divorce, remarriage, stepparents, etc.

In the coming chapters we will address both of these reactions with practical, helpful suggestions. But in the meantime let me encourage you that there are benefits from reviewing your family of origin. Even though the total picture is not yet clear, stay with it. Allow the material in this book and the care and concern of your friends to help you piece together the puzzle of your past. Understanding your past will help disentangle you from emotional hangovers you may be experiencing. You may be trapped in bitterness or you may be too dependent on others as an adult. Both situations are directly related to your family of origin.

I want to make two points. First, adult children often think that there is nothing they can do about the past. It is true that you cannot undo the events of your past. But you can certainly do something about your attitude about your past.

Second, it is possible that your family of origin is characterized by more than one family personality. You may identify

95

elements of both the Ruling family and the Protecting family in your family of origin. It is not unusual to see a mixture of two family styles. One parent can be ruling in nature, the other protecting. Your assessment of your family depends on which parent you were closest to and which parent was predominantly active.

Comparing Families

To help us gain understanding and perspective, let's look at the family portrait diagram on the next page. The purpose of this diagram is to give the big picture of how the five family personalities fit together on the individuality-relationship continuum. If you have difficulty finding yourself in one family personality, at least try to place yourself somewhere on the continuum. For example, you may generally identify your family of origin as somewhere between the Bonding family and the Ruling family.

Look at the portraits of the five family personalities. Notice that members of the Chaotic family are separated from one another. The kids tend to be reactive and/or abrasive in their personal relationships and extremely self-protective. On the other extreme, in the Symbiotic family, it is difficult to distinguish individuals because of the smothering parent. The children lack the psychological freedom to be individuals in their own right.

Keep in mind that there is no perfect family. However, the other three family personalities—Bonding, Ruling and Protecting—are closer to the proper balance between individuality and relationship. The Bonding family, which is the most balanced, shows a strong marital coalition and an effective communication network between the couple and their children. The Ruling family is mostly autocratic, with one adult in control. The short arrows between family members indicate a lack of expression of warmth and self-sacrifice. The Protecting family portrait shows one parent who tends to be too sacrificing for the children, which limits the development of their individuality.

Family Personalities

Chaotic · Ruling · Bonding · Protecting · Symbiotic

Individuality — Relationship

Extreme — Balance — Extreme

| Disengaged Alienated | Self-orientation over Relationships | Relationships Self-orientation and Relationships | Relationships over Self-Orientation | Entangled Fused |

I think and I'm Right You're wrong | I am probably right in my thoughts | Individuality I think and you think | I am not sure what your thoughts are | "we" think, we do not have our own thoughts

The next diagram demonstrates the cause/effect correlation between a parent's behavior and a child's behavior, highlighting implications for self-esteem and potential psychological problems. The descriptions of parent and child behavior are certainly not all-inclusive. However, parent behavior tends to program child behavior.

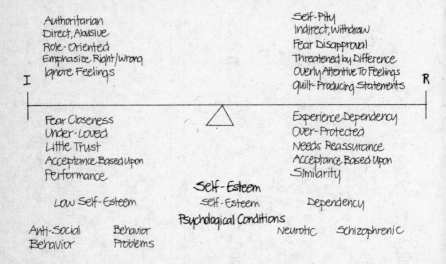

Children who grow up in Chaotic and Ruling families exhibit an elevated self-orientation. Those from Protecting and Symbiotic families struggle with dependency.

There is also a correlation between the family of origin personality and possible psychological conditions which express themselves in the adult child. Because Chaotic families are so antagonistic toward relationships, they may cause the development of anti-social behavior in their children. People with problems such as lying, cheating, stealing, and white-collar crimes often come from Ruling families. Neurotic difficulties like anxiety and depression are usually found in adult children from Protecting families. Chronic anxiety, depression, and schizophrenia are frequently related to Symbiotic families.

Marriage Personalities

What kind of marriage relationships produce these different family personalities? Here are brief descriptions of the seven marriage personalities followed by a diagram placing them on the family personality continuum.

Active-Passive: This is the most common personality (approximately 28 percent of all marriages). It consists of an aggressive partner (usually the wife), who diligently strives to make the marriage work, and a passive partner, who is led or directed.

Active-Resistant (24 percent): Consists of two talented, strong-willed individuals, one who is aggressively seeking closeness in the relationship and one who is actively resisting the effort.

Helper-Helpee (8 percent): This relationship is sustained by the fact that one person (the helpee) needs the other (the helper).

Macho (12 percent): One partner (almost always the husband) totally dominates this marriage.

Kids (5 percent): This is a marriage between two immature "kids" who are not ready to cope with the pressures of life. They need outside help, often from their parents, in order to survive.

Pretense (3 percent): This is the rarest category. It is a "make-believe" marriage between two people who have no romantic attraction to each other. They have totally different backgrounds, interests, goals, and values.

Active-Active (20 percent): This marriage is founded on a firm commitment to each other, and both partners are equipped and motivated to make the marriage work.[1]

---

[1]David Field, *Marriage Personalities* (Eugene, OR: Harvest House, 1986), p. 26.

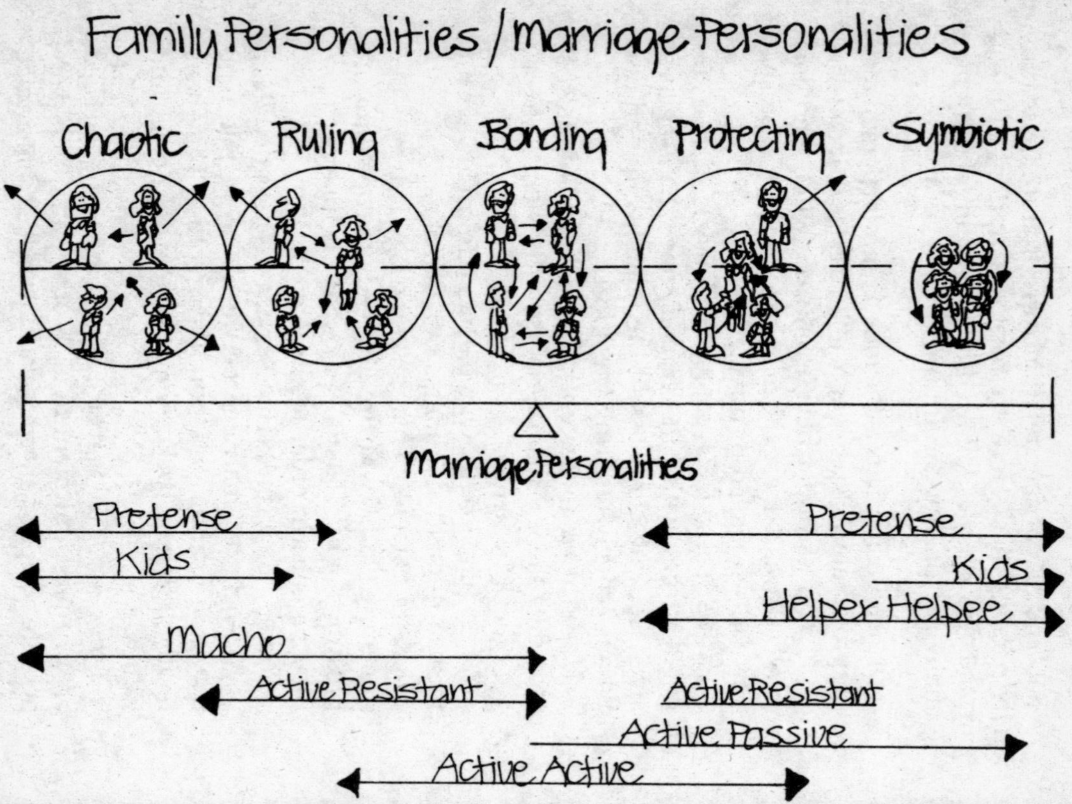

Family Personalities / Marriage Personalities

Chaotic   Ruling   Bonding   Protecting   Symbiotic

Marriage Personalities

Pretense
Kids
Helper Helper

Active Resistant
Active Passive
Active Active

Pretense
Kids
Macho
Active Resistant

Pretense marriages fit on both ends of the continuum and move toward the middle. Even though they do not have a solid marriage, some of these couples can work together as parents. The Kids marriages tend to be very uncontrolled and disorganized, usually located on the Chaotic side of center. Macho marriages are the same, though they extend more toward center.

Active-Resistant marriages develop into either a Ruling or Bonding family personality. Occasionally they lead to a Protecting family when one of the parents is detached from the marriage and children, and the active parent is very protecting and caring.

The Active-Passive marriage translates primarily into the Protecting family, with spillover into the Bonding family and sometimes the Ruling and Symbiotic families. The Active-Active marriage basically populates the Bonding family and moves into the Ruling and Protecting families.

Look and Listen

Again we come to the question of what to do with this new information. I have a few specific suggestions at this point. More will be offered in chapters 12 and 13.

First, you need to observe your behavior around others. Do you tend to give in to your children or do you become more determined and demanding when there are disagreements? Do you think about how others can help you or do you take care of your problems by yourself? Are you hostile toward your parents or are you afraid they are going to emotionally obligate you? One man commented, "Every time I talk about my father it is like a razor edge that makes spaghetti out of my stomach. I can't stand him." His wife said, "Every time I talk to my mother on the phone I give in to her opinions. It's like I'm still her little girl. I'm afraid to stand up for myself." Both are identifying the effects of their families of origin on them today.

Second, after you have observed your behavior and attitudes around others, consult with your spouse or an insightful friend. Tell them about your family of origin and where you think you fit. Ask for their feedback. If talking to others is difficult or impossible, I suggest that you write down your impressions. Remember: The very act of attempting to translate feelings and actions into words will help you be more objective about your family of origin.

So far I have sketched a picture of the five basic family personalities. For some of you, none of these personalities fit. There are some special kinds of family situations that require our attention because they are so traumatic to children. Perhaps one of the traumatic situations in the next chapter may describe your family of origin.

Traumatic
Families

– 9 –

Traumatic Families

Virtually every day we learn about a new family tragedy on the pages of the local newspaper or while watching the local evening news on television. The sad and sordid details vary, but one fact remains constant: Kids are the primary victims of these horrible, sadistic stories. They usually receive the worst physical and emotional bruises.

Often these sad stories happen in traumatic families. A traumatic family is any family in which certain activities or events significantly hinder the effective functioning of that family. Much of what the family talks about and does is influenced by these disruptive conditions. The traumatic family is an ongoing relationship that negatively affects the spiritual, emotional, and psychological development of the children. Traumatic families are literally imprisoned by a particular relationship problem or condition.

We will examine four kinds of traumatic families in this chapter: the alcoholic family; the hyper-religious family; the abusive family; and the disadvantaged family. If your family of origin does not match one of the families described in this chapter, you may still identify with some of the hurtful dynamics of one or more of the traumatic families.

The Alcoholic Family

John came to see me on the advice of his pastor. He looked much older than his 39 years. His eyes and his cheeks were sunken, and deep grooves creased his brow. His wild eyes moved back and forth like caged animals. Here was a sorrowful-looking man who had experienced deep inner pain.

John's wife, Kari, had given up on her alcoholic husband after 18 years of marriage. Scotch on the rocks had turned their relationship into marriage on the rocks. She still went through the motions of the marriage, but the love and romance were gone.

John described himself as "a selfish, male chauvinist pig who is hard on the people I love." Alienation was his middle name. Business acquaintances, friends, and his children were unable to get close to him. Rash decisions, caustic barbs, and broken promises spawned his reputation as a hard man without feelings.

When I probed into his childhood John spoke bitterly about an alcoholic father who frequently came home in a drunken stupor and beat John's mother. "I tried to stop him," John said. "But he just threw me out of the way. I hated him for what he did to Mom. I feel so guilty and angry that I couldn't stop him. I can still hear my mother screaming."

John began to sob as he continued to reveal the childhood he had tried to forget, but instead had unwittingly reproduced. "I would do anything to get my dad's attention, but he always disappointed me. He would come to my ball games drunk and embarrass me in front of my friends. One time I smiled at him and he busted me across the lip because he said I was making fun of him. Whenever he was around, Mom and I walked on egg shells. When Vietnam came along I joined the service because I couldn't stand to be around him anymore."

John had trouble making sense out of his present family life because his childhood family never made sense. Unfortunately John duplicated his father's behavior. He was an alcoholic and treated his wife and children the way he and his mother were treated.

The Alcoholic Pattern

John's story graphically illustrates the power of alcoholism to traumatize families. There is a direct correlation between alcoholism and marital dysfunction. Alcoholics abandon marital and parental duties, leaving their children without a positive model of normal family living. The family is captivated by the alcoholic and much of the family's energy is diverted into dealing with the condition.

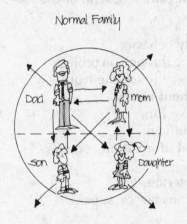

Normal Family

Mom and Dad are reciprocal in supporting each other and cooperative in supporting the children which encourages a child's development.

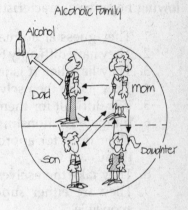

Alcoholic Family

Alcohol captivates Dad and the entire family. Children, instead of receiving support, fill in for Dad and help Mom.

There is rarely a strong marital coalition in alcoholic families. Consequently, what little parenting exists is usually one-sided. There is tremendous pressure on the nonalcoholic spouse (Mom in the diagram) as she attempts to hold the family together. Often she exacerbates his alcoholism by protecting him from the consequences of his drinking. The dependent spouse cooperates with and covers for the alcoholic for many reasons: To avoid public embarrassment; to avoid having to deal with change; or perhaps to punish herself for her own failures.

The spouse and the children of the alcoholic expend a tremendous amount of energy on his behalf. When he is "sick," they do his chores and lie to his boss and friends about his condition. Because the alcoholic requires so much attention, the children do not receive the attention they need from parents—love, play, and support in their activities.

Kids from alcoholic families often exhibit several of the following negative characteristics:

1. They guess at normal family behavior.
2. They have difficulty following through on projects.
3. They lie when it is just as easy to tell the truth.
4. They judge themselves without mercy.
5. It is difficult for them to have fun.
6. Intimate relationships are difficult.
7. Their need for approval and affirmation controls them.
8. They take themselves very seriously.
9. They are either super-responsible or super-irresponsible.

Adult children from alcoholic families often make these kinds of comments about themselves:

I am isolated and afraid of people.
I don't know who I am.
I am afraid of authority and personal criticism.
I feel like a victim and I am attracted to people with weaknesses.
I feel guilty when I stand up for myself instead of giving in to others.
I am addicted to excitement.
I tend to love people I can pity and rescue.
I have repressed my feelings from the traumatic events of my childhood, and I have lost the ability to feel or express feelings because it hurts too much.

I am terrified at the prospect of being abandoned. Yet I enter relationships with people who are never there for me emotionally, and thus I fulfill my fear of abandonment.

There are three rules which children learn by default in alcoholic families:

1. Don't talk. If you don't say anything you won't get into trouble.
2. Don't trust. If you don't rely on your alcoholic parent, you won't be disappointed.
3. Don't feel. If you ignore your feelings it won't hurt.

Adult children of alcoholics feel robbed of a normal childhood in their family of origin. It is a loss that cannot be replaced. They recount their embarrassment when childhood friends visited their homes, for they never could depend on the unpredictable alcoholic parents. They generally avoided their alcoholic parents, hoping to avoid embarrassing confrontations. They learned to deny reality and to lie—labeling Dad's hangovers as sickness.

Adult children of alcoholics have trouble with love and commitment because they didn't experience it in their families of origin. They experienced feelings and behaviors opposite of the norm. For example, they felt happy when their alcoholic dads left the house, whereas most kids feel disappointed when Dad leaves. Interpersonal relationships are a challenge and spouses of adult children interpret their behavior as disinterest or non-caring.

There are five issues that the adult child of an alcoholic must confront and resolve:

1. *Control:* They want to be in control of circumstances because they lived a life of unpredictability in their families of origin. They may also want to control people.

2. *Trust:* Depending upon somebody else is very risky because their experience over the years is that people do not tell the

truth. The child may think that his dad is drunk, but he is told that his dad is only sick. Therefore the adult child feels he cannot trust his own perceptions.

3. *Feelings:* As children they tried to avoid their feelings. So taking the risk and learning how to attach feelings to people and events takes effort.

4. *Need:* They tend to ignore their own needs and often cannot even identify their needs. They may try to live on the edge— little sleep, few or no friends, poor nutrition, and reckless driving. They do things that make them susceptible to a mishap.

5. *Denial:* They try to deny that their alcoholic family has any affect on them as adults. They do this by exhibiting a narrower than normal emotional range and little or no memory about particularly traumatic events of childhood. They display social apathy or cynicism, a short attention span, a sense of feeling overwhelmed, and difficulty thinking clearly.

There is no doubt that most kids are negatively affected by growing up in an alcoholic family. However, there are changes and adjustments that can be made. If you are an adult child of an alcoholic, you must stop escaping and start confronting the facts. First, quit ignoring the past and talk more openly about your family of origin with your spouse, a trusted friend, or a trained counselor. Second, when you know you are bothered by something but cannot identify why, don't ignore it. Try to express your thoughts and feelings on paper or to a friend. Third, attend a support group for adult children of alcoholics.

Coming to faith in Christ changed John spiritually but not mentally. That's because change takes time. John had been programmed as a child, then spent 18 more years practicing what he learned. He needed to be reprogrammed. He needed to develop a new way of thinking. John did this by getting involved in a men's Bible study. He let the light of Scripture shine into the dark inner chamber of his past. John's group held him accountable for his actions, and with their encouragement, he made some significant changes. It won't be easy to reverse the damage, but Kari is beginning to believe there is hope. Her husband is a better man today, and with God's help he'll continue to improve.

The Hyper-religious Family

Tina and Ted came to me because Tina had been carrying a bucket of thoughts, feelings, and pressures for her entire life. She did not feel acceptance from anyone in her immediate family, including her husband Ted, and she questioned her love for him as well.

As we talked Tina consistently mentioned that God had withheld His blessings from her because she was inadequate. It was obvious that Tina did not like herself, and she continually found fault with her actions and attitudes. She was caught in the trap of trying to please others. She feared what God would do to her if she did not help others. Enough was never enough. Her list of spiritual do's and don'ts was endless.

Tina was the oldest of six children. Dad was a stubborn, harsh man who insisted that the kids be involved in church activities. As the oldest child, Tina was expected to be a spiritual example to her siblings and the other kids in church.

Tina has always felt that she was on trial before God. She tried to do the right things but her fears persisted. The more she feared, the more she did things for God in an attempt to alleviate her fears. That's why she gave many hours each week to her church—on top of a full-time job—stressing her to the point of exhaustion.

As a child Tina learned many rules for "proper" Christian conduct. The first time she attended a movie she had difficulty enjoying it because she was afraid someone would tell her parents. As an adult she still has an overactive, hypersensitive conscience. The "rules" of the faith have locked her mind in a prison of oughts and shoulds. Tina still does not feel acceptable to God or others.

The Hyper-religious Pattern

The hyper-religious family is controlled and influenced by an extreme spiritual focus. This family traumatizes its children when it threatens them with the loss of relationship with their parents and God if they do not live up to certain spiritual rules. The parents are consumed by their fear of God's rejection and they transfer their fear to their children. Parents live under a divine mandate to make their children believe. They don't understand that they are to introduce their children to God without coercion.

The Pharisees of the New Testament are an example of the kind of hyper-religious activity that is destructive to children. The Pharisees were obsessed with rigid adherence to rules and standards instead of pursuing a loving relationship with Jehovah God. To them proper performance determined one's relationship with God.

Hyper-religious families are usually involved in religious settings that are extreme. Most often, excessive legalism dictates the spirituality of the group. But occasionally a family is hyper-religious due to the psychological weakness of one of the parents. Then religion becomes a tool to deal with personality shortcomings. For example, a very insecure person might find power in a cult and become intoxicated with his influence over others. He does not exercise religious power for the good of others but to meet his own needs.

Is it really possible for families to be so religious that they harm themselves and their children? I think so. For example, Harold became a Christian when he was 35. Harold is so thankful that Christ has changed his life that he wants the same for his family. Therefore, he insists that his children—ages 16, 12, and 10—attend church and follow a religious regimen that is totally foreign to them.

Harold's motivation is pure. But in his fervor to get his children to endorse his belief, he has become demanding and pushy.

He nags his kids about clothing, music, language, habits, and lack of interest in God. The children think Dad is obsessed with God. They are being alienated from Dad and from God. Ironically Harold's overemphasis on religious activity is splitting the family apart instead of bringing it together.

Over-spiritualizing can be traumatic for kids. Every conversation is laced with spiritual language. The daily newspaper is discussed like a spiritual commentary. The chore of cleaning out the garage is turned into a spiritual activity. Difficulty with the next-door neighbor is considered a sign from God to move. Every life event is filtered through a spiritual lens.

The spiritualizing parent harms his children when he claims they are out of tune with God if they do not interpret events in the same way he does. Children are forced to choose between agreeing with him and losing their individuality, or disagreeing and becoming more detached from him. In addition, older children often back away from the hyper-religious parent because they cannot relate to him.

Hyper-religious families are on a treadmill of failure and fear as they feverishly try to please God through performance. They perform for God because they are afraid of what He will do if they fail to perform. The normal, healthy religious person performs for God out of love as an outgrowth of what God has done for him. But kids from the hyper-religious family learn that there is no way for them to consistently please God. So they give up and detach themselves from all religious activity or become religious neurotics—frantically fearful of what God will do to them if they say or do the wrong thing.

Adult children from hyper-religious families of origin often function like religious robots. They walk around with a cognitive awareness of God, full of theological truth, but they have little spiritual life. They can spout all the dogma, doctrine, and traditions. But they experience no inner spiritual power.

In my counseling I find that adult children from hyper-religious families have extreme difficulty getting close to the Lord. They spend years sifting out the difference between religious do's and don'ts and God's unconditional acceptance. They want to believe God loves them, but they need help. The best thing they can do is get into a supportive group of Christians who will affirm them and help them experience God's love.

THE ABUSIVE FAMILY

The term abusive family seems incongruous. How can anyone abuse the people that he supposedly cares for? Yet we know it happens all the time. Those close to us often elicit some of our strongest emotions—including love, hate, and lust. Nearly half of the murders in the United States are committed within families.

Amy told me during counseling that her husband had been pushing her around. His abusive behavior related to her unwillingness to have sex with him. A few times he had ignored her disinterest and demanded sex, to which she finally consented.

After eight years of marriage Amy found sex repulsive. It seemed like the only time her husband was nice to her was when he made physical advances. When she suggested that he leave her alone for awhile, he responded, "I have left you alone for an entire week and it hasn't changed anything. Admit it: You just don't like sex. You're weird."

Amy really wanted a good marriage and a fulfilling sexual relationship for both of them. She despised what had happened to her and the marriage. She knew the blame was partly on her shoulders too; she could not reduce the problem to her husband's demanding behavior alone.

I asked Amy to tell me about her family of origin. She said her mother divorced her violent father when Amy was about nine. Two years later her mother remarried and the family seemed more stable and happy. But when I asked her to tell me about her junior high years, she stared at me as if her mind had gone blank. There was very little she could remember. We proceeded to high school years. She told me that she was a mediocre student and participated in a few activities. After high school

Amy moved away from home to take a job in a large city. She met her husband-to-be and, after two years of dating, they married.

I was curious about Amy's apparent loss of memory regarding her junior high years. I asked her to tell me about her neighborhood, her friends, the house she lived in, family activities, and schedules. I asked her about her mother and her stepdad—their marriage, their jobs, her relationship with each of them. She said that her mother worked evenings and that her stepdad stayed home with her and her brothers. "Did your stepdad ever come into your bedroom to talk to you?" I asked.

"Yes," she answered hesitantly.

I asked Amy to close her eyes. "I want you to imagine yourself back in your bedroom at night with your stepdad there. Can you see the room? Where is your dad sitting? What is he doing?"

Amy's voice began to quaver and her words were garbled. She started to cry, and then shouted, "No, no, no!" Then the words poured out, and the pieces of the puzzle came together. "I couldn't stop him. He kept forcing himself on me and there was nothing I could do. I couldn't tell my mother because it would ruin their marriage, and I didn't want to do that to her. But I lived in horror of going to bed at night."

Coming to terms with the reality that she had been sexually abused was a painful but necessary step for Amy. It was the beginning of a healing process in the inner core of her life. Amy made significant progress in the following weeks. It still was not easy for her to relate to her husband. But their relationship improved as she worked on regaining her wholeness as a person. Amy was further helped by her decision to become a Christian.

The Abusive Pattern

When we talk about the abusive family, we must consider not only sexual abuse but also physical beatings and verbal harassment. Each of these violations does long-term harm. They traumatize the child in that the relationship between the victim and the perpetrator is often destroyed. The child victim is not nurtured, but instead is used to satisfy the emotional and/or physical impulses of the victimizer.

The physical abuser has usually been abused himself. Often the abuser is hyper-sensitive—overresponding to a verbal or nonverbal cue. One abuser explained, "You looked at me funny and that's why I hit you." An insecure person handles perceived rejection from other family members very poorly. This insecurity leads to negative reactions which can result in physical violence.

Some abusers have no conscience. They are insensitive to the pain of others because they endured so much pain in their childhood. This person is especially mean and is looking for conflict. He will verbally taunt children and call them names. If there is any reaction by the victim, the abuser becomes a monster, attacking physically and verbally.

The abuser feels like other family members are weak, spineless liars. He suspects that other family members are against him and are secretly plotting behind his back. His temper is uncontrollable. He blames others to somehow excuse his own actions. And then he makes statements like, "I warned her and she didn't listen. She asked for it."

Adult children from physically abusive homes are tough and untrusting. They have been slapped, kicked, and punched for such reasons as a look, talking back, trying to protect another family member, or carelessly breaking a dish. Usually these adults despise their abusing parent and have no desire for contact. They can be victims as well as abusers in their own marriages. If they are not victims, at least they are constantly on-guard, feeling like the spouse is going to violate them in some way.

Sexual abuse sends repercussions across generations of families. A sexually abused child frequently has sexual difficulty as an adult. I have counseled men who were sexually molested at two years of age and are addicted to sex as adults. One grandfather, who was molested as a child by a relative, repeated the abuse with his own grandchild. Whatever the scenario, sexual abuse in the family of origin damages the sexual health of the succeeding family.

The most devastating aspect of child sexual abuse is the deep inner hurt resulting from betrayal by the person who is supposed to protect. After that kind of trauma, picking up the pieces presents a real challenge. The victim may replay the events over and over again. Often she feels condemnation for not saying or doing anything. Or she is haunted by the abuse, sometimes waking up terrified after a bad dream.

If you were abused as a child, you may have convinced yourself that there is nothing that can be done about it now. However, if you are plagued by sexual dysfunction or frigidity, or you are nonorgasmic in your sexual relationship, then you need to consider getting help.

I have a couple of suggestions for those of you who were victims of abuse as children. First, recognize that abuse victims have trouble being close to others. You may feel worthless and undeserving of any love. Do not attack yourself for the way you feel and act.

Second, you need to talk to someone about your past. This will help you get perspective on an intensely emotional life experience.

Third, realize that abuse can produce a tremendous amount of anger and resentment toward the abuser. The victim can easily get caught in the trap of living her entire life as a victim of resentment. Do not let the events of the past so control you that you are not the person that God created you to be today.

THE DISADVANTAGED FAMILY

Mary's seventh grade classmates called her "flea bag." She came to school in shabby clothes with her hair in a mess. She performed poorly in every subject except English. With her flea bag reputation, she was a loner. Who would dare be her friend?

Mary's family was very poor. Her father was a laborer whose paycheck barely covered rent and food. Her mother was a simple person who always seemed to be having bouts with her nerves. Her disheveled appearance was an embarrassment to Mary.

School was a nightmare for Mary. Mary felt so rejected and frustrated. As hard as Mary tried at school, things did not go well. She felt like a mistake and a social failure. About the only activity that gave her any comfort was reading. Her books were a temporary retreat into another world.

After high school, Mary found a job in a local factory. She began making enough money to improve her life-style. At age 20 she married a man from the factory. She and Barry worked very hard and saved their money, determined to provide a better life for their family than they had as children.

Occasionally Mary tried to help her parents. Her mother's bouts with nerves escalated over the years, ending tragically in a fatal overdose of medication. About a year later her father died from cancer.

The residue of Mary's childhood is still with her today. She will not leave her home unless she is "put together." She does not want to embarrass her daughter the way she was embarrassed by her mother. It is important to Mary always to have money available. When her daughter began experiencing academic trouble in seventh grade, Mary immediately hired a tutor.

Mary has kept her past to herself. Barry and the kids know a little through their limited contact with Mary's parents before they died. To Mary, there is nothing pleasant about her past that is worth recalling or talking about.

The Disadvantaged Pattern

There are hundreds of kids like Mary who never get much of a chance at life. Certain people who are poor, or who lack intelligence or athletic ability, or who are socially regressive often become social lepers. If they grow up in a disadvantaged or disorganized family, they are often beaten before they start. These children feel worthless, shy, and full of shame. Their crime is not being able to fit into the mainstream of society. In not meshing with others, they become social outcasts.

A disadvantaged family produces certain disadvantages for its children. For example, a child from a disadvantaged family will likely receive more negative attention when having trouble in school than a child from a stable family. Emotional and physical handicaps, low intelligence, chronic illness, pervasive poverty, or crime may also attend the disadvantaged family. The child feels scorned, but there is nothing he can do. He feels great shame that he comes from a disadvantaged family. It is difficult to develop a family legacy and personal esteem when society's subtle message is, "You're not very good; you're not worth much."

The disadvantaged family is either ill-equipped, untrained, or unable to meet the legitimate needs of children. Kids are absorbed by their own difficulties or trauma. Their incapacities leave them feeling defenseless, alone, and embarrassed. The disadvantaged child feels like he should apologize for being alive. The feeling of rejection from childhood peers and the community sticks with him for many years.

Adult children from disadvantaged families can compensate in a number of different ways. Some become "missionaries" to disadvantaged children because they can't forget their own pain. Others achieve position and accumulate possessions to guard against ever being embarrassed again. Many want to hide the past and close the door on their history.

If you have such a background, recognize that it is okay not to want to go back to the past. There is no merit in living in poverty, but be aware that security does not rest in things. If you try to make possessions your security, you may end up being controlled by things just as you used to be controlled by the lack of things.

The real challenge is to diminish your sense of shame from your disadvantaged background so that you do not spend your life compensating or apologizing for it. Believe it: Your worth as a person is based on something much more valuable than your station, accomplishments, or accumulations in life.

Counseling Can Help

One final note to adult children from all traumatic families: You may profit greatly from the help of a professional Christian counselor. I recognize that counseling is not a panacea for all ills. However, trained Christian counselors can provide objective and caring assistance.

For family of origin issues, it is usually best to find a counselor who has been trained in family therapy. Call a few local churches for referrals. Ask Christian friends about counselors they know. And check the yellow pages or phone directory. After you have developed a list of three or four counselors, interview them by telephone to see which might be best suited to your needs. Ask about their training, professional memberships, licenses, and counseling approaches. Ask them how they balance faith and therapy in their practices. And check the fee structures.

Tell them about your values and beliefs, and what you hope the counseling will accomplish. Ask the potential counselor if he/she can help you reach your goals within the framework of your values.

As you interview each therapist, your comfort level with their responses will guide you to a proper choice. Be careful of self-proclaimed counselors with little or no training, especially if they have no supervision. Once you have decided on a counselor, set up an appointment and be willing to work with him/her.

The
Divorced Family

– 10 –
The Divorced Family

Susan would never forget that day. It was a beautiful spring afternoon as she walked home from school under a bright blue sky and puffy cumulus clouds. Susan could imagine her mother's delight at seeing the straight A's on her report card. The back door squeaked—as always—as Susan entered. "I'm home, Mommy!" she chirped excitedly as she skipped into the living room. There sat her mother, weeping. The tears frightened Susan. "What's wrong, Mommy?" Susan asked.

Her voice broken, Susan's mother sobbed the shocking news: "Your father has left us for another woman."

After her dad left, Susan rarely saw him. Through her grandparents and others she kept up on his wanderings throughout the country, hearing about his periodic changes in jobs and women. Occasionally Susan received letters from him containing five dollars. But that was the extent of Susan's contact with her father. She considered him disgusting.

Susan's mother never fully recovered from the divorce. She spent her days in a housecoat doing nothing. Susan had to cook, clean, and help her mother make household decisions.

In high school Susan excelled in good grades and extracurricular activities. She was a very determined person; so much so that she scared off guys who wanted to date her. Her high standards could not be met by the guys she knew.

After seeing her mother suffer from lack of job skills, Susan's first priority for her life was a vocation. She also wanted a wonderful marriage and happy children. She hoped to gain sweet revenge on her father by parading her successful family in front of him without him being able to take any credit for it.

During college Susan met Terry. He was everything she wanted in a husband. And Susan's drive and determination—along with her blue eyes and big smile—appealed to Terry. Their relationship was on and off for the first year due to their strong personalities. Each of them found it difficult to trust someone else. But they settled into a steady relationship which calmed their fears, and they married following his graduation.

Initially every aspect of their life together went well. They moved to another state for Terry's first job. Susan finished school and excelled in her work, as did Terry. He started traveling in his business about the time their first child was born. That's when their problems started. After a week of fighting his way through airports, Terry was in no mood for house duties. He wanted to play basketball with his buddies. But Susan needed help at home because she had been on duty alone all week—working days and caring for their son at night. Susan and Terry's strong personalities collided regularly over the next few months with little resolution to their conflicts. Neither of them knew how to compromise.

Gradually Susan noticed that Terry was less amorous and more detached. She became suspicious of his traveling activities, but Terry denied any wrongdoing. She began to fear that her husband would do the same thing to her that her father had done to her mother. Susan's fear caused her to complain and accuse; she could not help herself. Every time Terry came through the front door she assaulted him with a barrage of suspicious questions. So he began to stay away from home more and more.

A year later Susan sat in her living room tearfully staring at the divorce papers from Terry's attorney. The one thing she feared the most and tried hardest to prevent had taken place. She was so angry at Terry she could scream; she was so hurt she wanted to give up. What good was life anyway? She had worked so hard and it had come to this. She looked at the picture of her son on the piano and wondered if he would repeat the pattern when he married.

Shock Waves

It is very difficult to measure the shock of divorce on the family Richter scale. We know that the tremors remain strong up to a year after the split. For many angry or disillusioned couples, divorce may be a reprieve. But for the child divorce is often the beginning of a lifelong sentence to pain. For many children divorce is like an amputation of an integral member of the family. The child's life does not end, but he can never reclaim his original family. Therefore, he must adapt to another kind of family whether he wants to or not. Some children adapt better than others.

Parents who divorce "for the benefit of the children" rarely benefit the children. Obviously there are situations in which divorce is the only option because all other avenues to marital peace have been cut off. But for many couples who divorce, it is a blatantly selfish act.

Divorce destabilizes children. A child may wonder if he is loved or lovable. Most children won't express it, but divorce produces a deep fear of total abandonment. If one parent can leave him, what is to prevent the other parent from leaving too? Children from a divorced family worry about the future, wondering what is going to happen to them. They are forced into a situation that they are not prepared to handle.

Adult children of divorce may carry fears of abandonment and loneliness into their own families. They often push their partners away from them with complaining, accusing, or smothering behavior. Their fear of divorce and reactive behavior against divorce can often produce divorce. Sometimes those from divorced families of origin leave their partners before their partners can leave them.

One of the most difficult assignments for children of divorce is maintaining loyalty to each parent. Most children have a strong desire and need to please their parents. They do not like doing or saying anything that may be construed as disloyalty.

When a divorce takes place, a child may feel pressured to choose sides, forfeiting loyalty to one parent. But often he doesn't want to drop his loyalty to one parent. So he squirms in a dilemma: How can he comfortably maintain loyalty to both if he knows they do not like each other? So he tries to maintain loyalty to both but tells neither about it. This leads to a condition I call psychological splitting.

A child needs to feel affection from and loyalty to his parents. However, in a divorce the child fears that he will risk loss of approval from one parent if he verbalizes loyalty to the other parent. To alleviate his fear, the child splits himself in order to hold onto each parent. One part of him is attached to Mom, the other part to Dad. But he does not allow his loyalties to mix, for fear of upsetting one of the parents.

For example, Rhonda, who lives with her mother, may feel very close to her father. But she is afraid that her mother will be upset with her if she displays her affection and loyalty for her father. Likewise Rhonda fears loss of Dad's approval if she tells him about a neat shopping spree she enjoyed with Mom. To be happy with one is to risk the loss of affection from the other. Children do not know how to navigate the troubled waters of joint allegiance. These kids split themselves in order to try to prove their loyalty to both parents.

Psychological splitting can be precipitated when one parent displays hatred for the other parent in front of the child. If Rhonda hears Dad put down Mom, Rhonda is not about to say good things about her mother to Dad. She does not want to risk Dad's rejection. She cannot talk to either parent about the situation; it is too risky.

Another dangerous situation for the child is taking the role of messenger or informant between divorced parents. Rhonda is interrogated by her father about the activities of her mother. The nosey father is manipulating Rhonda's loyalties. In order to prove her loyalty to her dad, Rhonda feels she is being disloyal to her mother by being an informant.

The role of messenger or informant often continues into the child's adulthood. If you are an adult child from a divorced family and are trapped in the informant's role, realize that being your parents' messenger is no longer your job. In fact, it never should have been.

Children of divorced parents often feel a tremendous amount of guilt. Many children think that they caused their parents' divorce by doing something wrong. They cannot escape the suspicion that the breakup is somehow related to them. The children blame themselves for being too ugly, too contentious, too much of a health problem, too irritating, or too bad. However, as the child matures the guilt should go away.

After a breakup, children often fantasize about their parents getting back together. Imagining a reconciliation is soothing for some. Fantasizing is also used to mitigate the pain of the divorce. Consequently when one parent announces plans to remarry, it can be very traumatic for the child. If Daddy marries another woman, then all hope of being together with Mommy and Daddy again vanishes. For some children it is more difficult to deal with the remarriage of a parent than with the divorce itself.

The Single Parent Family

What happens to family structure and family personality when a divorce results in a single parent family? The family personality may change. For example, suppose Dad is pushy and domineering, a Ruling family type of parent. But the couple is divorced and Dad leaves. Mom is more relationship-oriented. She does not like confrontations and she is tired of doing everything herself. The family is likely to shift from a Ruling family to a Protecting family personality. Now the children are faced with adjusting to different family personalities: a Ruling family with the exiting Dad, and a Protecting family with Mom.

Single Parent and Surrogate Parent

Children from about age 12 and up face another problem with the single parent family. Note in the diagram on the previous page how the departure of one parent often elevates the older child to the status of a surrogate parent. This replacement role means that the child is forced into adulthood sooner than normal. Life becomes too serious at a young age. He or she may face the uncomfortable task of supplying support and comfort to the single parent and discipline to younger siblings.

If Mom remarries, the surrogate parent/child faces another challenge: giving up the surrogate position. Once a child has gained a position of authority, whether he wanted it or not, it is difficult for him to give it up to an incoming stepparent. A remarriage, especially with older children involved from both families, can spawn some serious power struggles in a blended family. So children in a blended family are not only faced with adapting to new parental positions, but the likelihood of a new family personality.

Adult Children of Divorce

It is obvious that divorce affects the development of children. The balanced qualities of individuality and relationship germinate with greater difficulty in the soil of divorced families.

As the adult child of divorced parents, you may be able to identify with several characteristic symptoms which plague your present life. You may not be very happy with your life. You may struggle with poor health. You are more susceptible to nervous breakdowns. If you are a man, you may complain of generalized anxiety that comes and goes without any particular stimulus.

You are more prone to marital problems. Since you didn't have the benefit of witnessing a productive, healthy marriage, you have less life training in marital and family issues. Men who grow up in divorced homes tend to be less involved as fathers and less able to relate to others in their family. One man from a divorced family of origin assured me that he cared deeply for his present family. But his caring came across as extremely mechanical to his wife and children. To him, family was an institution, not a relationship. Little wonder: From age 12 on his "family" was a military academy.

You may also complain about pervasive, intense feelings of loneliness. You are particularly susceptible during holidays, weddings, funerals, and special events. Gaps in family affiliation persist, resulting in feelings of alienation from significant others—especially your parents.

Single Parent Family > Blended Family

What can you do if you are plagued by some of the symptoms just described? It is important to realize that these conditions and feelings are normal for your experience and history. Some of the effects of divorce will not go away completely. So it is very important that you identify your strengths and goals and move ahead despite your occasional feelings of discouragement or loneliness. You must put your past in perspective and move into the future. Chapter 12 will help you evaluate and deal with your past experiences with parents and stepparents.

Also I suggest that you release yourself from any feelings of responsibility you may suffer from the failure of your parents' marriage. You may need to seek professional Christian counseling to help you work through the maze of feelings you have carried into your adult life and family. You will also benefit by reaching out to others, such as children and teens who are presently suffering through a divorced family as you did. You have much to offer them. Furthermore, Scripture challenges us to utilize the comfort we have received to comfort others in tough situations (see 2 Corinthians 1:3-5).

Before we launch into ways of resolving those lingering issues about your parents, it will help to understand the methods that kids use to cope with their family of origin. Chapter 11 leads us into this helpful topic.

How Kids Cope

– 11 –
How Kids Cope

Let's suppose that you have been asked to to work on one of two committees. You attend the first committee meeting and are introduced as a new member. The chairman then announces the goal of the session and a lively discussion ensues. Several times during the conversation you contribute, and each time the other members listen to what you say. At the end of the meeting, the goal has been reached and you feel good about your participation and the warm reception you received.

The next day you attend a meeting of the second committee. No one introduces you, and there are no name tags to help you learn the other members' names. You introduce yourself to a few people, but they are not at all warm or cordial. The meeting begins and immediately several members start arguing. You're not sure what the committee is trying to accomplish, but it's obvious that people feel strongly about their views. Once or twice you try to interject an idea, but you are interrupted before you can say much. It's obvious that no one is interested in your viewpoint. When the meeting is over, you are frustrated because you realize the committee did not complete its agenda.

If you had to choose membership in only one of the two committees, judging from your first experience with each committee, which one would you choose? Most of us would choose to join the first, and elect to avoid the second, for obvious reasons. The first committee is filled with pluses, whereas the second committee is marred by minuses and question marks.

Unfortunately, unlike this illustration, children cannot choose their families. Neither do they receive advance information about their parents to know if their arrival will be welcomed or not. Apart from our confidence that God is sovereign, we might be tempted to believe that placement into a family is strictly a matter of chance: When your number comes up in the great baby factory in the sky, you get dumped into the next available family. But God sovereignly places us in our families of origin for reasons which are perhaps only known to Him.

After arrival, every child is faced with the task of learning how to cope with the family into which he is placed. Kids are not immune to their environments any more than seeds are unaffected by the soil in which they are placed. A child's family may or may not be conducive to growth. And for some kids it's not a matter of *growing* in the environment; it's a matter of *surviving* the environment.

Children in families with Chaotic and Symbiotic personalities and in traumatic families generally adopt one of six unhealthy coping styles. Elements of these coping styles can be found in any family. However, the more extreme the family situation, the more likely it is that a child will try to cope in one of these six ways.

The Responsible Child

The responsible child copes with his less-than-ideal family environment by going above and beyond the call of duty. He is the one who brings home decent grades and does the chores without complaining. He takes initiative around his parents and others. Parents and teachers love him. Usually the responsible child is very busy. He is like a little adult adapting himself to the standards of the adults around him. Of course, his actions gain him attention and reinforce his behavior.

Ron was a responsible child. As an adult he complained to a counselor about chronic lack of energy and low motivation. During the interview the counselor discovered that Ron had two younger sisters and a younger brother that he had always taken care of. Ron's mother never remarried after his father's untimely death. Ron had been the glue which held the family together, gaining him the respect of his community.

Shortly before seeking counseling, Ron had attempted to help the younger of his sisters reconcile with her husband. He was unsuccessful and, to Ron's dismay, his sister blamed him for the breakup of her marriage. Ron had always worked hard to help his sister. Her hurtful accusation sent Ron into an emotional tailspin which led him to the counselor's office.

Ron was helped considerably when he began to see his family of origin as emotionally handicapped. Before he died, Ron's dad never seemed to be pleased with Ron's work. Ron could excuse his father's rejection when he realized that his dad did not have some of the skills necessary to be more accepting. Ron felt that his dad did care for him, though his dad had not clearly displayed his caring before he died.

Ron discovered in counseling that he had longed for a normal family of origin much like an amputee longs for his lost limb. But Ron realized that all his longing could not recover that which was already lost forever. Instead of wasting time and energy pining over his loss, Ron had to accept his loss and go on. He had to deal with the fact that his father was not accepting and his sister was not appreciative.

Once Ron accepted his losses he could finally give up trying to be the perfect child, surrogate parent, and exemplary citizen. He realized that he was still trying to earn his father's acceptance even though the man was long dead. He also discovered that being too responsible for his sister had hurt her in the long run. He could finally allow himself to accept his own mistakes. He saw that, even if he was perfect, it was impossible to gain the appreciation from his sister that he wanted. Once he was relieved of this emotional tension, Ron's depression began to subside.

There are many adult children who are still trying to prove themselves to their parents. They are giving their parents every excuse to love and accept them. If their parents do not come through, then they try even harder. Some spend a lifetime trying to be good enough to please their parents. They are addicted to responsibility. But no matter how responsible they are, they will never command the affirmation they want.

The only solution to the dilemma of the responsible adult child is to give up trying to be perfect and start accepting self and family of origin as they are. I am not suggesting that these individuals become irresponsible. However, it is a mistake to try to buy love and acceptance from Mom and Dad through responsible behavior.

The Reclusive Child

The reclusive child has an exaggerated feeling of weakness, accompanied by real and imagined fears and a sense of emptiness. Reclusive children coped with their unfortunate family circumstances by escaping into an emotional cave from which they peer out at the world.

Carl was a reclusive child. His father left home when he was six months old. His mother was educated, verbal, opinionated, and selfish. She never remarried. Carl had little contact with his mother because she worked most of the time. They lived in the same house, but you could hardly call them a family.

Carl saw his father occasionally, but rarely for more than an hour at a time. Carl always wondered what his dad was like. He wanted a relationship with him, but his dad was inapproachable. Once, when Carl was about 12, his dad called on the telephone. Carl did not recognize his voice so he asked, "Who is calling?" His father was so offended that he hung up. Carl never heard from his father again. Ironically, Carl never told his mother because he did not want to hurt her.

As a teenager Carl craved relationships, but he also feared them because he was so unsure of himself. He felt like a social klutz, often retreating from social encounters to the safety of his bedroom. He participated in a few school activities, but most often he found himself working alone in the darkroom as the film developer for the yearbook staff. Even though isolation was not always comfortable for Carl, it was safe.

Carl's reclusive coping style overpowered most of his attempts at socializing as an adult. He wanted to be part of the group, but his preference for the safety of solitude sent him back to his condo to read the Bible, listen to music, and watch television. Fortunately, Carl became involved in some activities that proved beneficial to his social development. He volunteered for small group training at his church, took some tennis lessons, and joined a coed volleyball team. With success in these ventures, his temptation to retreat diminished and his social confidence grew.

The reclusive child may become so disillusioned with life that he escapes into unreality or commits suicide. Reclusive adolescents may choose these avenues when they are not successful dealing with the frustrations of a poor family situation.

The "Rambo" Child

Like the aggressive fictional character from the movies, "Rambo" children cope by attacking instead of retreating. These kids have exaggerated defense mechanisms. They dare people to love them, then laugh at them if they try. They are suspicious and reluctant to trust anyone. Usually they have grown up in a fairly hostile environment, often with an abusive parent. They are quick to act and they go for the throat—hurting others as they have been hurt. Trouble is a pattern of life evidenced by scrapes with the law and constant battles with their parents, siblings, fellow students, and, as adults, their spouses.

Rambo children usually come by their behavior honestly. Like playful puppies, these kids all started out innocent and harmless. But a puppy will grow into a vicious dog if it is constantly beaten, antagonized, and teased. Children who are persistently abused and tormented can grow into aggressive, hurtful adults

Adult Rambo children are secure when they feel a sense of power or control over others. They are so locked into winning and being in control that they push others away from them.

Thus they live in social isolation. Very few people feel safe around them. It takes a lot of energy to tolerate their abusive, caustic personalities.

If you are an adult Rambo child, the best thing that can happen is for you to lose your sense of control. Powerlessness can serve as a catalyst to bring about some changes in your life, such as spawning increased sensitivity toward those you presently hurt. The next step is to deal with your need for control which isolates you from others. When you must be in control, you are imprisoned by your own lack of trust. Your inability to trust torments you more than others.

How can you reduce your need for control? First, recognize that God is ultimately in control, not you. Second, ask yourself, "Can I be trusted by others? Am I a person who can be counted on to keep his word? If not, why not?" Third, experiment with your loved ones. When you are tempted to control them by what you say or do, back off. Catch yourself! Say to yourself, "I will allow him/her to be in control. I will trust God that everything will work out. Five years from now I won't care anyway!" And fourth, develop a more active relationship with Christ. As you do, your need for control will diminish.

The Manipulating Child

A cartoon showed two laboratory mice contentedly enjoying some food at the end of a maze. In the caption, one mouse said to the other, "You know, in a few more weeks we'll have these two psychology interns pretty well trained."

The manipulating child copes with his family environment in much the same way. Ostensibly the parents—like the interns—are in control. But in reality the manipulating child cunningly and deceitfully controls his parents, knowing just what to say and do to get what he wants. He will lie about others to make himself look good, and do so apparently without a twinge of conscience.

Manipulating children are usually spoiled. They often live in homes that are professional, cold, demanding, and materialistic. Social recognition, popularity, and possessions are very important to these families. Therefore, they deem it perfectly acceptable to do whatever they need to do in order to get their way, to look their best, and to have more things. Self-centeredness dominates as they use people to meet their needs. Manipulating children usually learn manipulation skills from one or both parents. They observe how their parents treat each other and how they manipulate outsiders to get their way. Then they turn around and use their learned skills on their parents

Because manipulation centers on deceit it appeals to the very basic, depraved elements of human nature. Sometimes only a hurt, a grave disappointment, or a traumatic event can break through the tough veneer of manipulation and selfishness. Manipulators may also be broken by someone who out-manipulates them, exposing them to the pain of embarrassment and loss of relationship. However, without intervention manipulators usually manipulate themselves into plastic relationships or loneliness.

The Conforming Child

Loretta excelled at doing what her mother expected of her. Mom was opinionated, domineering, and the major influence in the family. Loretta had always been a cooperative child. Grandparents, aunts, uncles, and cousins knew Loretta as the "nice one." She never caused anybody any trouble and always seemed to do exactly what she was told to do precisely when she was told to do it.

The conforming child differs from the responsible child. The responsible child takes initiative and hotly pursues acceptance. But the conforming child is more laid back, having learned that the way to acceptance is to do what people tell you to do. The conformer prefers comfort and avoids argument.

There may be a price to pay for the comfort, however. By allowing herself to be told what to do, Loretta developed a habit of not acting for herself. One day, as a young adult, it suddenly dawned on her that she was tired of being told what to do by her mother. Conformers like Loretta may revolt. However, they often do so by conforming to someone who is the opposite of their parents. A revolt can be even more dangerous than remaining under the tutelage of Mom and Dad.

Conformers sometimes become upset with themselves because, by conforming for acceptance, they sell themselves short. If Loretta tries to tell her parents how she feels, they are shocked. Her mother may respond, "Loretta, what's gotten into you? You've never acted this way before!" Loretta's attempt to establish a separate identity is discounted. She has conformed to them so long and so well that they refuse to accept her in any other role than her conforming role.

The adult conforming child may need to separate herself from her parents in order to shed the conforming role. Initially such distancing creates discomfort for the child and the parents. However, if negotiated properly, it can yield some very positive results. The conforming child must speak her mind, whether or not her parents agree, and expand her circle of contacts beyond the family.

The Irregular Child

Some children cope with their family environments by believing that they are irregular—misfits, factory seconds, rejects, good-for-nothings. Rene was such a person. Her parents were divorced when she was only four. Her mother was turned in for child abuse many times before the divorce. At seven Rene was adopted by other relatives. Her adoptive mother was also turned in for child abuse, and her adoptive father abused Rene sexually. In adolescence Rene was sexually molested by two other men in her adoptive family.

As a teenager Rene attempted to reconcile with her mother. But her mother told her she did not want Rene back and never wanted to see her again. Because of the abuse by her adoptive parents, Rene returned to her natural father, who had remarried. Since she had not lived with her father for eight years, Rene did not relate well to him, or to any man for that matter. Her stepmother, though a kind person, was suspicious of Rene and accused her of creating problems with the couple's younger children.

Rene had trouble relating to people her own age. She said that she felt odd when she was with other teens. At 17 there was hardly anything left for her. Abused physically, used sexually, rejected by her natural mother, adoptive parents, stepmother, the school, and three employers, Rene was at the bottom. She saw herself as an irregular person with little value.

Rene needs a number of friends—people who will stick with her regardless. She needs the love of others who will reach into her world of rejection. Convincing Rene that she is not a reject will take time. She has been rejected by so many for so long that she expects people to reject her. In fact, she is so convinced that she is irregular that she will play the role until you reject her like everyone else has.

In order to move beyond her irregular style, Rene must *want* to move beyond it. Her challenge is to risk being accepted despite past rejection. Of course the key player in alleviating her struggle is the Lord. Accepting His love will help her learn to accept the love of others.

If you are still coping as an adult irregular child, you must accept yourself as a person who is loved and accepted by God, not as an irregular reject. You must focus on God's love for you and begin to act in this positive manner.

Coping Styles Are for Children

Did you exercise one or more of these six coping styles as a child? If so, remember: Coping behavior is excusable for kids, but not for adults. Continuing to operate these coping mechanisms into adulthood can destroy your marriage and your children.

When the Corinthians were first converted, Paul did not criticize the new converts for their fleshly condition because they were new in the faith. However, after a period of time he confronted them, telling them it was time to grow up and stop acting like children. Similarly, I do not think anyone can criticize a child for coping with a traumatic or dysfunctional family environment in any way necessary. Kids have to survive in whatever way they can. However, as an adult you must confront these childhood coping mechanisms. They are not good for you or the people close to you. Confronting long-standing coping styles is not easy, but consider this: If you coped once as a child, you can learn to better cope as an adult. The next few chapters should help you in that process.

Facing
the Past

– 12 –

Facing the Past

It's been said that those who ignore history are destined to repeat its mistakes. We've noted so far that our families of origin have a significant effect on our lives today—particularly our present family relationships. The patterns of our parents' marriages and parenting styles are often repeated in our own marriages and the parenting of our children. Sometimes that impact is positive; many times it is not. So it's important that we each face our past and deal with it in order to understand our present. Then we'll be better able to make any desired changes.

Remember Susan in chapter 10? She was the woman who grew up in a divorced family. She was so determined that her marriage would succeed that she ended up driving her husband away. John, described in chapter 9, had a similar experience. He was deeply hurt by his alcoholic father, yet he duplicated his father's abusive behavior with his own wife and children.

Before Susan and John could begin to resolve their problems with their own families, they needed to face their families of origin. Understanding their past helped them determine why they acted as they did in the present. And that understanding of the past and present motivated them to change.

Gaining insight into the family of origin is helpful for all individuals, not just for those with problems. When you have faced your family of origin—whether good or bad—you are better equipped to preserve and enrich your relationship with your children. Conversely, if you allow your past family to intimidate you, it is likely that your children will be intimidated by you. Acknowledging and incorporating your past into your present will benefit you, your spouse, and your children.

Facing Your Past, Present, and Future

Facing your past means accepting that your family of origin is an integral part of you; it is the foundation of your life. Many adult children exit their families and never process their childhood experiences. They see no purpose in dredging up the past, so they isolate it in a separate compartment of their thoughts and fail to integrate it into their present lives. So they avoid seeing themselves as affected by their families of origin, yet they operate in their present families based on how they were programmed in their previous families. This chapter will assist you in the process of responsibly evaluating your family of origin.

The Parent Evaluation, which I will encourage you to complete later in this chapter, is a tool which will help you capture your thoughts and impressions about your parents. Evaluating your relationship with your parents in this way will greatly clarify your understanding of their impact on your present life and family.

There are three terms in the Parent Evaluation which must be discussed first so you can answer the related questions appropriately. The terms are triangulation, family labels, and double binds. Understanding these attributes is vital to understanding your past. Consider these parenting behaviors in regard to how you were treated as a child, and how you treat your children.

Triangulation

Triangulation occurs when parents demand from their children what they are missing in their marriage. In a triangulated family, both parents use the child as their go-between, or one parent establishes the child as a replacement for his spouse. In a triangulated marriage, children become the marital glue. Mom and Dad keep their marriage alive through the triangulated child.

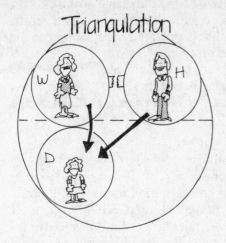

Triangulation

Parents' relationship blocked
Mother and Daughter relationship
heightened — Daughter is
triangulated
Dad is partly connected to
Daughter but more distant
than the mother.

Ward was distanced from his wife, Faye, but he was still emotionally attached to his daughter Abby. Kept at arm's length by her husband, Faye devoted her emotional energy to their children, but predominantly to Abby. The couple fell into the habit of negotiating their marital conflicts through Abby. In some ways Faye used Abby, the triangulated child, to replace her emotionally distanced husband. Faye attached herself to Abby in place of Ward. Abby was caught in between her parents and she felt responsible to preserve their marriage.

This situation persists even though Abby is now an adult. It is obvious to Abby that Mom and Dad do not get along with each other. But they both get along with her. She is informally appointed as the sustainer of her parents' marriage. Abby's unnatural role in the marriage causes her much confusion and stress.

What can Abby do to relieve this pressure? The only solution is for her to stop playing their game. When Faye starts talking to Abby about her father, Abby must interrupt and say, "Mother, I will no longer be the go-between for you and Dad. If you have a problem with Dad, you need to talk to him about it, not me."

Abby may also inform Ward, "Dad, Mom tried to talk to me about some problems between you two. I told her that she needed to talk to you directly. It is not my responsibility to get involved with your marriage problems."

Abby's stand on the issue will be a shock at first. Ward and Faye are used to having Abby as their buffer. They will probably test her resolve. But she must persist for her good and theirs.

Family Labels

Family labels are the nicknames, bywords, or descriptive tags parents use to identify their children. Labels can be positive or negative, either stimulating or discouraging for the child. Some typical labels are sunshine, honey, clumsy, rebellious, sweet little girl, self-centered, capable, talented, potential, and dumb. Once parents label their child it is difficult for the child to escape that identification.

For example, Johnny's parents constantly complain to him about being strong-willed and stubborn. Their complaint is intended to persuade Johnny to change his behavior. But the label only reinforces Johnny's behavior. He hears himself called stubborn and strong-willed so often that he assumes the label is his identity and he continues to act out who he is.

At times parents subconsciously attach labels of negative behavior to their children so they will not have to change or adapt themselves. For example, what would happen to the family if Johnny was no longer strong-willed and stubborn? The equilibrium of the family would shift, forcing the parents to relate differently to Johnny, and vice versa. If parents don't blame Johnny for the problem, they might be forced to recognize and deal with their ailing, unhappy marriage.

Sometimes a parent uses labels in an attempt to externalize his own internal conflicts. Johnny's father is also stubborn and strong-willed. Therefore, when Dad disciplines Johnny, Dad is really disciplining himself. And the father who says to his teenaged son, "You aren't a man!" may be questioning his own manhood and punishing himself by yelling at his son.

What is a child supposed to do when he is negatively labeled by his parents? It is difficult to be on the receiving end of a parent's projected needs, especially when that parent is still needed by the child. If the child conforms to the parent's label, both the child's behavior and the parent's image of the child are reinforced. Eventually the child assumes the identity behind the label he has been given.

As an adult, Johnny may still see himself as stubborn and strong-willed—perpetuating the label from his family of origin. But if he still behaves in a stubborn and strong-willed manner, it is now his job to deal with it. Johnny needs to realize that the labels he received from his parents in the past are not binding in the present, especially if those labels are causing him problems as an adult. He does not need to perpetuate negative labels in order to prove his loyalty to Mom and Dad, even though the temptation is great to remain unchanged.

If you are an adult child who is still acting out your parents' negative labels, you need to start using positive labels for yourself. List five personal strengths. If you can't think of five, ask a few friends to identify the strengths they see in you. From that list select the five you most want to work on. As you concentrate on affirming and developing those positive traits, you will find that the effect of the negative labels from your family of origin will diminish.

The Double Bind

The double bind is a sophisticated, subconscious, and effective method of controlling children. However, this method is destructive to kids. Often a double binding parent is afraid to face the adult world, or he fears being abandoned by his children. Consequently the fearful parent establishes an unhealthy, entangling bond with the child. The double bind is an intimate but restrictive relationship. The parent prevents others from entering in and prohibits the child from getting out.

The double binding parent constantly accuses the child of not caring for or appreciating him. In response, the distraught child repeatedly tries to prove to the parent that he really does care. However, the parent discards the child's efforts by accusing the child of not being sincere.

In the double bind relationship the parent has persuasive power. The child's whole world and self-view is controlled by the parent. The youngster questions his own identity and is confused about reality. He may think he shows his love, but the deceptive parent insists he does not. It's the parent's word against the child's self-perception. And since the parent is the authority figure, the child concludes that he must not love his parent like he thinks he does. What is worse, the child begins to doubt the validity of his own thoughts and feelings in light of his parent's controlling authority.

Here's an example of a double binding parent manipulating her relationship with her child. Mom approaches little Kevin and he reaches out to give her a hug. But Mom hesitates and pulls back slightly. Wanting to please his mother, Kevin also hesitates, thinking Mom doesn't want a hug. Then Mom asks accusingly, "Don't you love your mother?"

Kevin has blown it again. He thought he was cooperating but, according to Mom, he was not. He can't win. If he insists, "Yes, Mom, I do love you," then Mom will chide him for not giving her a hug. Disagreeing with the controlling parent produces anxiety. The child's poorly developed ego can hardly stand the rejecting, accusing tone of the parent. So the child rarely objects.

For the adolescent of a double binding parent, leaving home is tremendously difficult. Symptoms of psychosomatic illness are common at this stage. Some adult children never escape this parental trap, and its controlling effects are terribly disruptive to the marriages of both the child and the parent.

Let's look at another scenario. Dad complains to his son Rick about a chore the child avoided. So Rick completes the chore, and then Dad complains about how poorly the child did the job. Dad has locked Rick into a no-win situation. Rick is criticized for ignoring the chore, then criticized for botching the chore. Most children can tolerate occasional incidents like this, but a steady diet injures a child emotionally, giving rise to constant self-doubt or reactive rage.

For the adult child who is trapped in a double bind relationship, the obvious solution is to separate from the parent. The adult child does not need to totally abandon the parent in order to affect a healthy separation. Rather, sufficient distance must be placed between them so that the child is no longer vulnerable to the parent's accusations. To do this, the child must develop his own internal gauges—confidence in himself and what he perceives. So when mother says, "Don't you love your mother?" he will recognize her attempts at manipulation and continue to love her his way. He will realize that he does not need to explain his actions or get emotionally hooked by her accusations.

If you were subjected to triangulation, family labels, or double binding as a child, perhaps your adult relationship with your parents has been very frustrating. You may still be storing a reservoir of negative emotions. Hopefully this information and the Parent Evaluation exercise will help you be more objective about your relationship with them. Use these resources to transform your existing, painful relationship into a relationship which is enriching and fruitful for you, your parents, and your present family.

Parent Evaluation

The purpose of the Parent Evaluation is to help you verbalize your awareness of and attitudes toward each parent. Take a few moments now to complete the exercise below. Then share your answers with your spouse or a close friend.

At the conclusion of this exercise you will find a sample Parent Evaluation which was completed by Marie, a client of mine. You may find her comments helpful as you complete the exercise.

Parent Evaluation

Write 10 descriptive words for each of your parents. You may use words from the list below and/or any others you may think of.

DAD	MOM
1.	1.
2.	2.
3.	3.
4.	4.
5.	5.
6.	6.
7.	7.
8.	8.
9.	9.
10.	10.

happy	witty	moody
worrier	heavy eater	temper
understanding	sad	optimistic
saintly	inexpressive	disciplined
materialistic	weak	brave
mean	sense of humor	outgoing
depressive	habits	good friend
caring	hard worker	boring
careless	tight	hypocrite
dependable	coward	adventurous
dry	quiet	excitable
drunk	angry	listener
lazy	religious	pessimistic
insensitive	giving	strong
deceitful	wimpy	

Write your general impressions of each parent. Include step-parents if they played a prominent role in your life.

What did/do you like about each parent?

What did/do you dislike about each parent?

What were/are their strengths?

What were/are their limitations?

Identify positive feelings you have toward each parent.

Identify negative feelings you have toward each parent.

Which parent are you more like? How are you like him/her?

What problems and/or obstacles did your parents face that affected their parenting?

Are you closer to one parent than the other? If so, why?

What traumatic events occurred in your family?

What was your coping style, if you had one?

Were you triangulated? If so, how?

Did your parents have an uncomfortable label for you? If so, what was it?

Did you feel trapped in a dou le bind? How?

What was your family personality? Explain.

Describe your general impressions of your parents' marriage. How is it similar or dissimilar to your marriage(s)?

Describe your relationship with your family of origin as a child and an adult child.

Would you like your relationship with your parents to be different? If so, how?

Marie's Parent Evaluation

Marie completed the Parent Evaluation when she came to my office for counseling. She complained about emptiness in her marriage and she was tired of everyone telling her what to do. Marie is 36 years old. She has been married 14 years and has three children. She works part-time in a dress shop. Her parents were divorced when she was 10 and her mother remarried two years later. Her father's drinking was the main cause of the divorce.

Write 10 descriptive words for each of your parents. You may use words from the list below and/or any others you may think of.

DAD	MOM
1. *happy*	1. *temper (hasty)*
2. *temper (slow)*	2. *materialistic*
3. *understanding*	3. *outgoing*
4. *brave*	4. *hypocrite*
5. *caring*	5. *excitable*
6. *very hard worker*	6. *angry*
7. *tight*	7. *pessimistic*
8. *semi-dependable*	8. *strong*
9. *distantly loving*	9. *insensitive*
10. *stretches truth*	10. *rather inexpressive of good feelings*

Write your general impressions of each parent. Include step-parents if they played a prominent role in your life.

My real father was an alcoholic when I was growing up, and because of that I didn't see much of him. He'd tell me to lie about the places we'd go so my mom wouldn't start a fight when we came home. I felt he loved his booze more than me. Now I understand that he was trying to show me a good time.

Mom hated my dad, and still does. Every time I came home from his place she made me wash, saying he was filthy. She was mean towards me. She doubted my actions, and still does. She was over-protective and accusing. I can't remember her saying she loved me.

My stepdad always worked hard to make my mom happy. He usually was pretty fair with me. I'm sure it has been tough for him.

What did/do you like about each parent?

Dad—He's what he is, take him or leave him.
Mom—Tough cookie; I wish I had some of that personality.
Stepdad—Sense of humor.

What did/do you dislike about each parent?

Dad—He didn't keep in touch.
Mom—She forgets that other people have ideas, thoughts, and, most of all, feelings.

What were/are their strengths?

Dad—Strong enough to give up booze.
Mom—Showed little emotion; cried on cue.

What were/are their limitations?

Can't really think of any.

Identify positive feelings you have toward each parent.

Dad—He loves me in a way that shows he cares and will always be there, even though we are not involved in each other's lives.
Mom—Right now I have a hard time finding positive feelings toward her because I am trying to break away from her. I guess she was always trying to protect me from harm from my dad and friends. But now I get hurt easily.
Stepdad—He always managed to stay happy even though he's been through some rough times.

Identify negative feelings you have toward each parent.

> *Dad—He didn't get in touch with me for a long time.*
> *Mom—She never lets me make my own mistakes.*
> *Stepdad—He never stood up for himself.*

Which parent are you more like? How are you like him/her?

> *I'm more like Dad because he is kind of a free spirit. I'd like to be more free, but I have no wings.*

What problems and/or obstacles did your parents face that affected their parenting?

> *My mom and stepdad, my real dad, and the loss of our home by fire.*

Are you closer to one parent than the other? If so, why?

> *I'm closer to Dad because I can love him and he never makes me feel guilty like my mom does by accusing me.*

What traumatic events occurred in your family?
What was your coping style, if you had one?

> *I think I conformed.*

Were you triangulated? If so, how?

> *I was more like the flag in a tug of war.*

Did your parents have an uncomfortable label for you? If so, what was it?

> *Sweet little Marie.*

Did you feel trapped in a double bind? How?

> *Yes, by trying to live up to Mom's expectations. It was hard to have fun or let my parents know I had fun, so I had to pretend.*

What was your family personality? Explain.

> *Symbiotic.*

Describe your general impressions of your parents' marriage.
How is it similar or dissimilar to your marriage(s)?

*My parents always had to be better than the Joneses. Mom always had
the last word to all of us. Their marriage included a lot of socializing and
entertaining. I was never allowed to make my own choices.*

*In my marriage, the biggest difference is that our kids are trusted. We
do more things as a family. We don't force each other.*

Describe your relationship with your family of origin as a child
and an adult child.

*I spent my life saying "please" and "thank you"—conforming.
When I tried to make a decision, the whole family turned on me like I was
crazy. They put guilt trips on me.*

Would you like your relationship with your parents to be different? If so, how?

*I would like my mom to quit smothering me and telling me how I
should feel and what I should do. Some day I think we will get along
better as I continue to learn how to deal with her.*

The information on Marie's chart is revealing. Even though
she and her father were not together much, she apparently feels
closer to him and safer with him than her mother. Marie is
obviously very frustrated with her mother. She sees her as a
tough, hypocritical, guilt-producing, and over-protective person. There is every indication that Marie's mother is still a
controlling, Symbiotic parent. Marie resents the fact that her
mom would not let her make her own mistakes.

Marie's label in the family was "sweet little Marie." That tells
us that she coped with her circumstances by conforming. Marie
identifies her family as a Symbiotic family personality. Note the
similarities between Marie's chart and the Symbiotic family
profile in chapter 7. Mom, the strong parent, did not recognize

the boundary between parent and child and was over-involved in her daughter's life.

What Marie identified as her major problem—her marriage—was a smoke screen covering the root source of her difficulty—that she was the product of a Symbiotic family. Once she understood that fact and began establishing a healthy self-identity, she was better able to relate to her husband. Marie's relationship with her mother is still very challenging. But there is improvement. She is learning to resist her mother's smothering control.

Becoming Peers
to Your Parents

– 13 –
Becoming Peers
to Your Parents

Twenty years had gone by. I had graduated from college, married, fathered three children, and lived in four states. During those years I had never spent more than one week at a time with my parents. Then they moved into our community for two months. They came to our home frequently. I met them for meals and stopped by their home after work to visit with them. Knowing them as parents was nothing new. But relating to them as peers—my friends—*was* new. When they moved away I said good-bye to two friends who also happened to be my parents. The two-month experience left me with a stronger sense of family heritage which I wanted to pass on to my children.

Adult children need to become peers to their parents. Otherwise they are locked into a parent-to-child relationship. Becoming a peer to your parents means that you establish an adult-to-adult relationship. You shift from relating to them as a child to relating to them as an adult.

We might compare the peer relationship concept to a union where there are both journeymen and apprentices in training. Once the apprentice is trained and obtains journeyman status, he is no longer an apprentice. The trainer-to-trainee (parent-to-child) relationship shifts to a journeyman-to-journeyman (adult-to-adult) relationship. Of course, the former apprentice has not achieved the same level of expertise or experience as the seasoned journeyman, but the two have the same status within the union. The new member now learns to relate to his former trainer as a friend instead of a boss.

Similarly the adult child is no longer an apprentice in the family but a full member relating to his parents as an adult. It is most important for you to act out the adult role with your parents, even if they continue to relate to you as a child. As an adult peer, treat your parents as you would treat other adult friends, but with the added respect which is due them as your parents.

As I enjoy an adult-to-adult relationship with my parents, I am grateful for what our example provides for my children. It is a more valuable inheritance than material items such as a new car or a college education. It is something that cannot be purchased. I am showing them what it means to be a part of this family. They see a model of how to maintain family relationships. As they see me relating to my parents, they are instilled with hope that they will be able to relate to me in like manner when they are adults.

The Family Conference

As a part of the process of building an adult-to-adult relationship with your parents, you would benefit from a family conference with your mother and father. If you're like most adult children, you want to care for your parents and resolve current and past difficulties. If your relationship with your parents is strained, you want to fix it, but you don't know how. You may even think it's hopeless. The plans and resources for a family conference provided in this chapter will help you accomplish your goal.

The purpose of a conference with your parents is to reestablish or strengthen a peer relationship with them in which they are both your friends and your parents. By *conference* I mean sitting face to face with your parents to discuss your pleasant memories, express your appreciation, and ask for feedback. If necessary, attempt to work through chronic problem areas and/ or current difficulties. A conference is a time for opening up and/or strengthening lines of communication between you and your parents.

I have outlined in this chapter a plan for a structured conference with each of your parents individually and with both of them jointly. Very few families converse with each other at this depth in our society, but almost every family needs it. Do it for yourself, for your parents, for your children, and to honor the Lord. Many parents are far more receptive to this kind of encounter than adult children may believe.

Before we get into the conference procedure, I want to alert you to three areas which you must consider as you prepare for a parent conference: what your conference can accomplish; some concerns about the conference; and a reminder that parents are people too.

What Can the Parent Conference Accomplish?

At least five positive results can be achieved in a parent conference:

1. *Increased cooperation.* Often parents are mistreated by their adult children when they are blatantly ignored, used, or passively excluded. A parent conference can encourage a deeper caring relationship between you and your parents because you are demonstrating your interest in them. And caring opens up wider avenues of cooperation between all parties.

2. *Increased dignity.* Sometimes our dealings with our parents are reduced to certain family occasions which are traditional or contrived. We only seem to have time for them when our attendance is required for some family function. It is time to move beyond such plastic behavior. Getting together with Mom and Dad for a straightforward conversation will restore their dignity as parents whose kids are eager to hear them out.

3. *Resolved issues.* The parent conference provides an opportunity to lovingly discuss with your parents past or current issues that cause you concern or dismay. During the conference you can explain your feelings and propose some solutions.

4. *Diminished remorse.* After their parents' deaths, many adult children wish they had spent more time talking to them while they were alive. Some adult children who have lost their parents carry around unanswered questions and unprocessed feelings.

Parent conferences can provide a time and place for these important exchanges and diminish the potential for remorse at our parents' passing.

5. *Energized grandparenting.* Your children need and can profit from interaction with your parents (their grandparents). Grandma and Grandpa have much wisdom to share from their life experiences. In many cases grandparents reinforce the teaching and positive influence of the parents. The parent conference can produce a conducive atmosphere for grandparents to positively influence your children.

Concerns About the Conference

You may resist the idea of a parent conference because of one or more of the following concerns:

1. *Negative results.* You may think that a conference will make your relationship with your parents worse instead of better. That's not likely. When approached genuinely, honestly, and without attack, most parents will respond in kind. If your relationship with them is fractured, try an informal approach at a slower pace.

2. *Dumping session.* Perhaps you fear that a parent conference may reveal something you did not want to know. Your parents may tell you things about yourself or themselves which you prefer left unsaid. To allay this fear, set some ground rules for the interview. Let your parents know that you will not dump on them and they should not dump on you.

3. *Forfeited security.* By becoming a peer to your parents, you are in the process of giving up your childhood. You are giving up the option to depend on your parents as those who are appointed to take care of you. You may wonder how you are going to handle the loss of security. This may be one of the first concerns you will want to discuss with your parents.

4. *Intimidating confrontation.* Some adult children will resist a conference with their parents because they do not want to sit down face to face with them. They are afraid of the actual

encounter or the results of the encounter. Such an exaggerated fear of your parents usually indicates that they intimidate you. Giving in to their intimidation by not contacting them only reinforces your fears and isolates you from one or both of them.

5. *No change.* There is always the possibility that a conference may not change anything between you and your parents. A conference may be helpful to you, but it may not improve your relationship with them. Difficulties may remain. You may not want to face the fact that your best effort to reclaim a bond with your parents was not successful. But remember: At least you made an attempt. Without it no progress could have been made. So an attempt is a success.

Parents Are People Too

Parents usually try to do their best for their kids. Most parents want their children to enjoy a better life than they did. Their intentions are positive. But we must realize that many life issues and problems get in the way of being a good parent. Parents are not perfect; they will occasionally succumb to the pressures of life which tempt them to compromise their best parenting intentions.

It is important to recognize that your parents had other demands and interests besides you—jobs, marriage, hobbies, their own parents, and other children. And your parents had their own questions about life, their significance, their worth, and their own personal fulfillment. Balancing the demands of being a parent, a partner, and a person was a challenge to them, just as it is for you.

Your parents did not choose their temperament, personality, or family of origin. They were recipients of these characteristics just as you are. They may have grown up in a home environment that severely hindered their personal development. And their childhood—good or bad—influenced how they parented you.

Parents are vulnerable, particularly to the pain of having hindered or hurt their children. Imagine the pain felt by a parent who recognizes that he contributed, directly or indirectly, to the demise of his child. That can prompt excruciating inner grief that is hard for anyone to bear.

And then we should recognize that some parents should not be parents. Dangerous parents do exist and they destroy or greatly hinder the healthy development of their children. There are some adult children who know exactly what I am talking about. Your childhood relationship with your parents was horrible. In many of these cases I would suggest that you not have a conference with your parents without the added assistance of a trained counselor or pastor.

Conference Procedure

Obviously, just having a conference with your parents is not going to establish you as peers or friends. It is a beginning or a reaffirmation of your adult-to-adult relationship. A conference will help you get to know them a little better, update your relationship, and make plans for the future.

As you prepare for your conference, ask the Holy Spirit to give you insight into your parents. After all, He knows them much better than you do. Also, pray about your obligations to your parents. The Bible tells us to honor them. How do you plan to honor them? A parent conference is one way. While you are preparing for the conference, ask the Holy Spirit to empower you to forgive and/or to foreclose on any negative feelings that you still may be carrying.

Review your Parent Evaluation from chapter 12 with your spouse. Together think through the parent conference. Rehearse what you need to say—especially in regard to what you want to see develop in your future relationship with your parents. Consider how the outcome of your conference may affect your own marriage relationship.

Now you are ready to contact your parents. Say to them something like this: "Mom and Dad, I need your help. There are some things about my past that I would like to find out about. I wonder if we could sit down and talk about my life with you when I was a child and our relationship today. It would mean a lot to me to find out more about you."

Assure them that you do not want to point an accusing finger or find fault. Instead you hope to learn about the past and how it applies to their present relationship with you, your spouse, and your children. Suggest that, the next time you are together, you would like to set some time apart for these talks. If the relationship is strained, meet in a neutral location.

What can you do if your family of origin has changed due to divorce, remarriage, and/or death? I suggest that you have your first conference with the family with whom you had the longest living arrangement as a child. For example, let's say you grew up with your mother, who divorced your father when you were eight and married your stepfather when you were ten. Meet with your mom and stepdad first. Then arrange a subsequent conference with your natural father.

What about meeting with your siblings? I think you should schedule a parent conference without inviting siblings. But above all, use common sense to determine your approach to your family in your unique family situation.

Individual Interview

The first step in a parent conference is to meet with each of your parents separately for one-half hour to two hours. Choose a location for the interview which is both comfortable and private. A neutral site may be desired, such as a restaurant or park instead of either of your homes.

You, the adult child, are responsible for the agenda of the individual interview. The primary purpose of this meeting is to get to know each parent as an individual by asking questions and inviting open discussion. Start the interview by sharing what you hope to accomplish. Set a positive tone for the meeting. Use any or all of the following questions as a part of your interview. Feel free to pursue any issues that come up as you proceed with the interview. You may want to tape the interview for future reference.

> What special memories do you have about your childhood?
> How did you get along with your parents?
> What did you like and dislike about your parents?
> What were your hurts and disappointments as a child?
> What were your hobbies and games?
> How did you usually get into trouble?
> What did you enjoy about school and its activities?
> What were your pets?
> What did you dream about doing when you grew up?
> Did you like yourself? Why or why not?
> What were your talents, awards, and achievements?
> Did you have a nickname?
> Who were your close friends?
> What would you do on a hot summer afternoon?
> Describe the area where you grew up—people, neighborhood, etc.
> What were you afraid of?
> How did you get along with your siblings?
> Who did you date?
> What was your spiritual life like as a kid?
> How has being an adult changed you?
> What have been your greatest disappointments in life?
> If you had your life to live over again, what would you do differently?

The secondary purpose of the individual interview is to give each parent feedback. Let each of them know that you appreciate and respect them. Talk about your hurts, frustrations, and unanswered questions.

Take out your completed Parent Evaluation and talk about your general impressions of each parent from your childhood. If there are issues to resolve, approach each parent with them at this time. Be specific and to the point. Talk together about what each of you would like in your future relationship. Invite the parent to read the page you wrote about yourself and your relationship with your family of origin.

Joint Interview

The second step in the parent conference is to meet with both of your parents together. The purpose of the joint interview is to relate to your parents as a couple and to receive their general impressions of you as a child and as an adult child.

To prepare for the interview, ask yourself these questions: What unanswered questions do I have about my childhood? What, if anything, do I need to resolve with my parents? What would I like to say to both of them that I have previously avoided?

Use the first set of questions below, and any others you may think of, to get your parents talking about their marriage.

> How and when did you meet?
> What was your first impression of each other?
> What was happening in your lives at the time you met?
> How did your parents respond to your dating and engagement?
> How did you decide to marry?
> What was your honeymoon like?
> What have been the strengths and weaknesses of your marriage?
> How did you get along with your in-laws?

Take a few moments at this point to share your general impressions of your parents' marriage using your completed

Parent Evaluation. Then continue the interview by asking questions about your parents' parenting experiences.

> What was it like to have children?
> What did you like and dislike about being parents?
> What are your general impressions of my siblings?

Take some time here to share your impressions of your parents' parenting from the Parent Evaluation. Talk with them about the personality of your family of origin and how you determined which personality best described your family. Then continue the interview by asking your parents about yourself and your role in their family.

> What are your general impressions of me?
> What were your hopes and dreams for me?
> What has satisfied you and disappointed you about me?
> How have I changed as an adult?
> What improvements would you suggest for me?
> Which of you am I most like and why?

Ask about events and situations you never understood or that were difficult for you (e.g. traumatic events, triangulation, sibling preferences, etc.). Talk about what kind of relationship you would like with them in the future. Ask them what they would like and how it can be accomplished. If it is appropriate, close the interview with prayer together.

While interviewing your parents about their marriage and parenting, you may uncover areas of difficulty between them, or between you and them. This is a natural time to talk about misunderstandings and hurts. However, it is important that you not judge your parents or their behavior. Ask them questions which will help you understand their perspective. For example, "Mom and Dad, it seemed to me that you overlooked how my brother picked on me. It really bothered me that he got away with so much. What was going on from your vantage point?"

Sometimes adult children want to know why their parents made them do or not do certain things. Were they too busy? Were there pressures that diverted their attention? Were they ever aware of this need? This interview can help to eliminate or neutralize some of your negative, harmful attitudes.

Remember that the primary purpose of the conference is to build a peer relationship with your parents. So use the following words of Scripture as a guide for your conference behavior:

> Therefore each of you must put off falsehood and speak truthfully to his neighbor, for we are all members of one body. "In your anger do not sin": Do not let the sun go down while you are still angry, and do not give the devil a foothold. . . . Do not let any unwholesome talk come out of your mouths, but only what is helpful for building others up according to their needs, that it may benefit those who listen. And do not grieve the Holy Spirit of God, with whom you were sealed for the day of redemption. Get rid of all bitterness, rage and anger, brawling and slander, along with every form of malice. Be kind and compassionate to one another, forgiving each other, just as in Christ God forgave you (Ephesians 4:25-27,29-32, NIV).

A conference between an adult child and his parents can impact all parties in a positive manner. I can almost guarantee that your efforts will further your peer relationship with your parents. But a successful parent conference is dependent upon your initiative, energy, and faith. The very act of meeting with your parents is an evidence that you see yourself as their peer.

Exceptions

You can have a parent conference without structured interviews. You might do so casually by asking some of the key questions over two or three informal visits. This approach has more appeal to some because it seems more manageable than a formal interview.

What if your relationship with your parents is very uncomfortable? There could be a severe breakdown in your relationship because of past or present circumstances. If you came from a Chaotic family, you will probably find it more difficult to engineer a conference than someone representing another family personality. Amy, from an abusive family, is very reluctant to meet with her mother and stepfather. Obviously there are many other traumatic and dysfunctional families which would make a conference either difficult or impossible.

In these cases I suggest, instead, that you review the parent conference questions on your own, then discuss them with your spouse or a counselor.

If your parents are deceased, you still need to bring closure to your past. An alternative would be to use stand-ins for your parents—their former friends, their neighbors, and/or other family members. Ask them to tell you about your parents, their perspectives, and opinions.

Then write a letter to your deceased parents. Tell them what you would have said in person. On occasion, adult children have gone to their parents' graves to read the letter and deal with the past. It is very appropriate to take your spouse and/or a good friend with you as a witness and a comforter.

Pointers for Peers

How do adult children determine if they are becoming peers to their parents? They know they are peers when they have accepted their parents as they are and have given up the need to change them. The adult child has become a peer when he does not need Mom and Dad's approval or cooperation. Peers act responsibly and do not blame their parents for their life problems. This does not mean that adult children give up hoping for change in their parents, or that they do not appreciate parental approval. It just means that adult children are complete whether or not parents change or give approval.

For example, let's say that an adult child, Tony, has always wanted his dad to tell him that he was proud of him. For years Tony has waited for a pat on the back and a congratulatory statement like, "I'm proud of you, Son." Tony has been upset and angry that his father has been cold and uncaring.

Tony becomes a peer to his dad when he no longer needs his dad's approval and no longer holds the lack of approval against his father. That doesn't deny that Tony would still like his dad's approval, but he no longer needs it in order to have a relationship with his father. He sees his father in a different light, realizing his limitations. Maybe he observes that his father showed approval in other ways. Or maybe Tony realizes that his dad really does not care and never will. He accepts the fact that he is not going to change his father.

Becoming a peer means giving up the dream of what your parents should have given you and accepting what you actually received. It means accepting the fact that their way of loving you is their way of loving, as unloving as it may feel to you. Do not try to make them be what you need them to be. Come to the point of enjoying them for who they are, even with their limitations. Accept their good and their bad points.

Honoring Your Parents

Honoring your parents means demonstrating respect for them spiritually, socially, and within your family. This does not mean you always agree with them or are not bothered by what they say and do. But you honor them by listening to them, considering their ideas, and confronting them as friends. You respect their family position, their skills, their hurts, and their privacy. Obedience is not required from the adult child, but respect is. If you cannot respect them as persons, you should at least respect their position as your parents. Honoring your parents is acknowledging the positive and letting go of the negative.

The Scriptures assert that honoring parents is a command from God, not an option. Specifically God calls upon us to care for our parents. Care can be supplied in a number of areas: physical, financial, medical, social, and spiritual. Care means meeting any need which the parent is incapable of meeting by himself. God's directive for you to care is not contingent upon how well or how poorly they cared for you.

Jesus clearly mandated that adult children are not to speak evil of their parents (see Matthew 15:4). Filial responsibility requires the adult child to refrain from criticizing his parents in public. Nowhere are we obligated to hold warm, gushy feelings toward our parents. For some that would be nearly impossible. But we can demonstrate honor by not making a public spectacle of them regardless of our feelings toward them.

Honoring also involves your attitude. Some adult children are skilled at honoring their parents with external behavior, but their hearts are hostile or cold. Christ said, "These people honor me with their lips, but their hearts are far from me" (Matthew 15:8, NIV). How do you honor Mom and Dad internally if you feel numb and resentful toward them? Be honest with yourself and with God about your feelings. But don't stop there. In addition, make a *choice* to honor them apart from how you feel about them. You can still honor your parents even if you are in the midst of unresolved issues.

Another way to honor your parents is by doing the best you can with your life. It is not a matter of trying to surpass your parents. Reaching your potential honors them.

Recently my teenaged son and I were playing one-on-one basketball. He has wanted desperately to beat me for a long time, but I have always been a little bigger and better. But the tide finally turned. His daily practice, long arms, and six-foot, one-inch frame were a little too much for good old dad. We had a great time banging the boards and doing our best to outmaneuver one another. But when it was all over he had beaten me 10-9.

After the game he said, "I've always wanted to beat you, Dad. But it wasn't as much of a kick as I thought it would be."

The "kick" for me is seeing him do his best at basketball and anything else he does. I feel honored when I know my children have done their best. In the same way I know it is an honor to my parents when I do the best I can. And, interestingly, honoring our parents in this way also brings honor to God.

Breaking
the Cycle

– 14 –
Breaking the Cycle

Most adult children want to do the best parenting job possible. But for some parents, productive parenting is a real challenge, considering the spillover effects of their families of origin. Adult children from poor families of origin tend to reproduce the harmful parenting skills of their parents. They are locked into a generational cycle, unwittingly repeating their parents' mistakes.

Diane, from the Symbiotic family in chapter 7, wants to know how to break the cycle. How can she parent more effectively than she was parented? In counseling, she has worked through her feelings regarding her parents and has developed her individuality. Now she wants to direct her efforts toward her two pre-adolescent children.

Bill, from the Chaotic family in chapter 6, also is desperate not to repeat the cycle. Like many adult children, Bill has openly declared, "I don't want to make the same mistakes my parents made." However, there is a strong possibility that Bill will repeat his parents' poor patterns. Even though the patterns are repugnant to Bill, they are all he knows about parenting. By being so determined *not* to do what his parents did, he is prone to subconsciously imitate them. Bill says to himself again and again, "I will not hit my kid." But because his subconscious hears "hit my kid" so often, he repeats the pattern and hits his 16-year-old just as he was hit by his father.

Breaking the cycle takes more than determination. And a negative focus (telling yourself what you are not going to do) will not work either. Face up to it: You are going to make some mistakes and repeat some patterns. However, you can compensate by engaging in some positive parenting behaviors. This chapter will help you break the negative parenting cycle by giving you three specific, positive "to do's": Model a stable marriage; foster a proper self-image; and balance individuality and relationship.

Model a Stable Marriage

The most important element in breaking a negative parenting cycle is a healthy marriage. Children prosper in an environment where Mom and Dad have a positively functioning and fulfilling marriage. A strong marital coalition is fundamental to healthy three-generational families. Ironically, this cornerstone of parenting does not even focus on the children. Positive parenting is a by-product of a positive marriage. When Mom and Dad are getting along, stability permeates the family. Children are free from the anxiety caused by marital tension, and the parents have more energy to parent.

Whenever a couple comes into my office to seek counseling about a rebellious child, almost invariably the root problem is an unhappy, unstable marriage. Initially I attempt to stabilize the child's unacceptable behavior. But my primary goal is to energize the marriage. A helpful first step to breaking a bad parenting cycle is to evaluate your marriage. I recommend that you complete the Marital Assessment Questionnaire found in my book *Marriage Personalities* (Harvest House).

One young prodigal father recognized the importance of breaking the cycle. After running away from family responsibilities, he returned home to his wife and children. He expressed his feelings to me in this poem:

> He's much too young to understand
> The feelings of a man,
> With troubled heart and jumbled mind,
> Who left his home and ran.

He thought he had lost
Another home, to find
The love he sought was always there.
How could he be so blind?
His hardened heart was almost closed;
His mind said, "Don't look back."
Then came the voice of one small boy:
"Is my dad coming back?"
His mother reached out one last time
To try to save our life.
But for the voice of one small boy,
I'd have never heard my wife.
So God, I pray, when oft it seems
That he is such a bother,
Remind me of the joy he brings
Each time he calls me "father."

I realize that a good marriage for a single parent is more or less out of his or her control. The circumstances that brought you to single parent status are likely unfortunate. And there may be little or nothing you can do about it now. So don't worry about it. But don't make things worse by putting your child in the middle between you and your former spouse. That leads to psychological splitting in your child. As a single parent your main task is to be a positive model for your children. Exemplify the behavior you want them to employ.

If yours is a blended family, the marriage needs regular and continuous reinforcement. The diagram on the next page shows that, in an original family, marriage takes place first and serves as the foundation for parenting. The horizontal line distinguishes parents from children. However, in the blended family the parent-child relationship for one or both parents predates the marriage and often is more powerful than the marriage relationship. In the diagram of the blended family, the vertical line shows the married couple divided, severely hampering

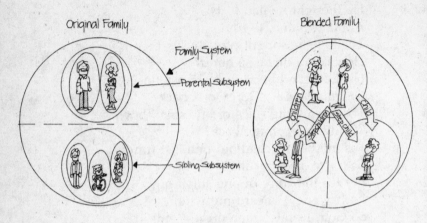

Natural Parent and Children vs. Natural Parent and Children
Commitment to children is more powerful than
commitment to the marriage.

family stability. Often the new marriage is secondary to existing parent-child relationships. The best thing parents can do for their kids is to make their marriage top priority.

Want to break the cycle? Build your marriage!

Foster a Proper Self-image

Your children came to you prepackaged. Think about it. You, as a parent, had nothing to say about your child's physical features, basic health, intelligence, birth order, or personality. But you do have some significant influence on your child's self-image. What is proper self-image? It is a person's self-judgment. Everyone has an image of himself in relation to his characteristics, strengths, weaknesses, and attributes. This image is the opinion that an individual holds about himself. It is a condition that represents his overall self-view.

A proper image seems to be derived from the quality of the relationships that exist between the child and those who play a significant role in his life. Children are experts in nonverbal communication. A child responds to the facial expressions of the parent. What happens when an adult smiles regularly at a young child? Usually the child begins to smile back. The child reflects what he sees in his parent.

Have you ever been to a house of mirrors at a carnival? Once inside, you stand in front of many mirrors. Each mirror gives you a different image of yourself. If you want to be skinny, stand in front of the "skinny mirror" and you look skinny. Wiggly, weird, oblong—there's a new image with each mirror. Suppose a person's first view of himself was in the house of mirrors. He might think that the distorted image projected from one of the mirrors described what he really looked like.

In your family, you are your child's first "mirror." A child's view of herself is your view of her as reflected in your words, actions, expressions, and voice tones. A child's self-image is what she sees reflected back to her from her parents.

A young child has no guidelines for making a judgment about herself. Consequently she depends upon the judgments of others. She doesn't know any better. One child is continually exposed to the scowls and frowns of her mother's angry face. Another child constantly receives her mother's smiles, warm eye contact, and soft touch. It is likely that these two children will come away from their encounters with different self-images. The first will see herself as inadequate or bad because she perceives anger or disapproval in her "mirror." The second will see herself as adequate or good because of the approval and acceptance her "mirror" reflects. Each will reflect the image which was placed in front her.

You have the opportunity to foster your child's healthy self-image by placing the proper images in front of them. Here are six guidelines for fostering a proper view of self.

1. *Display acceptance.* Acceptance implies that you like your child and accept her as she is. Acceptance does not require a child to be more than she is. Exhibiting interest in a child and involving yourself in her world demonstrates acceptance. A

child craves to know that her parents approve of her as an individual.

Does displaying acceptance for a child mean that you should not have expectations for her? No! The problem is that most parents are pretty good at expressing their expectations, but fall short in expressing acceptance and approval. As a parent, make mental notes of your child's positive traits and actions and communicate your approval.

Unrealistic parental expectations have shipwrecked more than one child's view of self. A child does not question whether parental expectations are fair or realistic. Rather, he questions his adequacy when he falls short of his parent's expectations. He thinks there is something about himself that is bad or wrong. And his self-doubts set him up for more failure.

It is critical for a parent to evaluate honestly what he is expecting of his child and why. Occasionally parents do not clearly verbalize their expectations when training their children in a task. And when the child fails, the parent criticizes or disciplines instead of accepting the child's attempt and clarifying the instructions. When the child fails, corrective action needs to be taken within an atmosphere of loving acceptance.

If I asked you, "Do you expect your children to make mistakes?" you would likely answer, "Of course!" But do your kids ever get a "freebie" mistake? Do they ever get the privilege of making a mistake without hearing about it from you? Being constantly picky and critical alienates your children from you and from a positive self-image.

2. *Provide opportunities for choice.* Decision-making allows a child to exercise control over his life and to explore his own interests. Making choices contributes to a child's sense of individuality. Opportunities for choice should be created and supervised by Mom and Dad based on the age of the child. For example, a six-year-old may not have the option of selecting any food item she wants from the restaurant menu, but her parents could allow her to choose from three options.

Once a child has made a choice, it is important to let him live out the consequences of his choice. By allowing your children to choose, you demonstrate your trust in the child. He can make decisions and, even if the decisions are not the best, you back the child. Bailing kids out of their bad choices does not teach them healthy choice-making.

3. *Set standards of behavior.* Parental standards for a child's behavior are a blessing in disguise for every child. Without rules a child has no fences around him. He lacks feedback on appropriate and inappropriate behavior. A child's individuality develops when he evaluates his performance against certain guidelines or known standards. So it is important for parents to establish specific limits and rules of behavior so the child knows what is expected of him and what is not permissible. Discipline is in order when the stated guidelines are not heeded.

4. *Foster optimism.* When parents employ a positive outlook on life and radiate confidence for meeting life's challenges, the children are instilled with optimism. A child's optimism is also nurtured when his parents help him evaluate a personal defeat in order to figure out a way to turn it into a victory next time. Optimistic parents can help a child turn a failure or partial success into a learning experience.

5. *Plan successful experiences.* A child's self-confidence is built when he feels some sense of mastery over his world. Ongoing achievements contribute to a child's sense of significance and capability. Parents are faced with the task of assessing a child's talents and planning activities in those areas which will lead to her success. Programmed successes will feed the child's confidence.

Children are involved in some activities where their choices are limited—school, for example. School involves academics, athletics, and social interaction. A child's success, or lack of success, in these areas may affect his self-image. It is a parent's responsibility to help the child deal with areas of weakness by encouraging him in areas of strength. For example, if a child is only mediocre in academics, his parents will want to help him compensate by excelling in an area of strength such as athletics or art. It is important to guide a child to attempt tasks and activities in which eventual success is certain.

It is crucial that adolescents experience success. Nonproductive and nondirected activity is a funeral dirge for many adolescents. Don't let them sit for hours in front of the tube, listen endlessly to their radios, and only do what they think is fun. Why? Because they miss out on experiencing the success which will build their self-esteem. They need to be tested in the laboratory of life experiences so they can discover new arenas of success. You do your teens a great disservice by letting them out of the lab.

6. *Listen*. Listening to your children means more than just hearing them. Listening is the activity of receiving words and pondering their meaning. Let your child finish what he has to say without cutting him off with a hasty "no!" or tuning him out because you have heard it all before. Good listeners also pick up nonverbal cues such as tone of voice, facial expression, and body posture. Listeners maintain eye contact and focus on the talker, attempting to understand his world.

When a parent listens to his child, he is saying to the child, "You are important to me. Agreeing with each other is not the issue. I respect your thoughts and feelings." Good listeners are much more likely to get invited into a child's world than tellers who do not listen. Listening promotes the development of a child's relationship skills. It teaches them to hear out and respect another person whether or not they agree with each other. Many family conflicts would be eliminated if the emphasis in communication was on listening instead of opinion-giving.

Listening is not always convenient. It may mean taking your teenager out for coffee on Friday night after her date. Sometimes parents need to take advantage of those moments when children (especially teenagers) are in a talkative mood. Parents who listen to their children at the early ages will have a far easier time listening to their teenage children because their children have confidence in them. However, it is never too late to start listening.

Balance Individuality and Relationship

As we have seen, the goal of parenting is to deliver your child into adulthood with healthy, balanced doses of individuality and relationship. Use these two concepts as reference points for the decisions you make and actions you take in regard to your children. Ask yourself, "How does this decision develop/affect my child's individuality?" and "How does this decision develop/affect my child's relationships?"

The best time to develop a child's capacity for relationships is when he is young. The parents' focus for young children should be on nurturing closeness, caring, and support. In adolescence the focus begins to shift toward developing their individuality. The child needs to more clearly define himself as an individual and take on personal responsibility. The diagram on the next page pictures the process that should take place as children mature.

A child's individuality and relationship are balanced when he has an accurate self-view and is able to relate to others. He respects others without losing sight of who he is. He acts on his own convictions while still acknowledging the convictions of others. He does not need the approval of others.

Children have souls. As a Christian parent, you must recognize that your active example of faith has immense influence on your children even though you may not see results in the short run. Be aware also that as your child is introduced to Christ, he is coming face to face with the One who is even more interested in developing his capacity for individuality and relationship than you are.

Notice that three of the guidelines for fostering a healthy view of self—choice-making, standards of behavior, and successful experiences—support the development of individuality. The remaining three—acceptance, optimism, and listening—promote relationship. If you feel that your child is underdeveloped in individuality, emphasize choices, standards of behavior, and successful experiences. Generally adult children from Symbiotic or Protecting families need to work on developing individuality because that quality has not been fostered in their background. Adult children from Chaotic or Ruling families will need to emphasize relationship. To do so they should concentrate on acceptance, optimism, and listening.

The first step in breaking your negative parenting cycle is to deal with your family of origin. Then engage yourself in a three-pronged effort with your children. Give them the privilege of living in a home which models a good marriage. Foster a healthy self-image by using the six guidelines I mentioned. And develop the balanced qualities of individuality and relationship in your children.

For many parents, struggling with their children may force them to deal with problems they experience with themselves, their parents, and their marriages. Right now you may feel alienated from your children and/or your parents. If so, it is time to reconnect. It is never too late to break the cycle. I wish you well in your journey.

— APPENDIX —

Guidelines for Dealing with Parents

These guidelines are not exhaustive. They are intended to help you interact responsibly with your parents, who may or may not respond positively. The critical issue is not their response but your responsible behavior with them. To a degree then, there is satisfaction in knowing you have done what you can.

Basic Rules

Rule One: Be direct. Many family members find it very difficult to be direct with one another. Instead, they pout, complain, shout, sit in silence, moan, or give confusing nonverbal cues. For example, your parents are visiting you and you notice that Dad has been quiet, keeping to himself. You may be on edge because you don't know if his aloofness is the result of something you did or said, or possibly his medication. What do you do? Sit down next to him and ask for his help. "How can I help, Son?" he may respond.

"Well, Dad, it seems to me that you have been quiet and removed in the last day. Is there something bothering you or am I just imagining things? Can you help me out with this?" A direct approach seeks to clarify the situation and resolve any misunderstandings. It does not attack.

You can be direct by being somewhat indirect: "How can I tell you, Mom, that your advice-giving really bothers me?" You are being direct with your mother but in an indirect way by recruiting her help. The message is delivered, but in such a way as to hopefully engage her in conversation.

Rule Two: Retain primary loyalty to your spouse. When a person marries, he shifts his loyalty from his family of origin to his spouse. It is up to each spouse to protect the marriage even if it means putting up barriers to protect against over-invasive parents.

Rule Three: Deal with your own parents. The parents and the child have a history together, therefore the message between them has more meaning than messages between in-laws. For example, Sally's announcement to her parents about holiday plans will carry more weight than if her husband, Jeff, tried to tell them. Sally may need support from her husband, but she is the best one to deal with her own parents.

The arrows that extend outside of the marriage circle show Sally and Jeff dealing with their own parents. The arrows inside the marriage circle demonstrate that they support one another.

Rule Four: Clarify gift-giving. It is certainly acceptable for parents to give their children money, advice, gifts, and other forms of help. Many parents do so without expectations. If you are suspicious that your parents'gift has hooks, clarify their expectations.

Do not continue to receive gifts if they feed an over-dependency on your parents. If your parents' gift-giving locks you into a child's role, the arrangement is preventing you from growing up. You must learn to take care of yourself apart from your parents' generosity and they must cooperate.

Rule Five: Family visits need agendas. Each family has its own rules or ways of doing things. When family members are together they generally need to adjust their rules in order for the visit to go smoothly. Partial planning helps family members make those adjustments because they can anticipate activities and the expectations of others.

Before the visit, discuss and decide with your family some things you want to do. An agenda can include daily routines, special activities, and time allotted for others during the visit. If family members know what to expect, and what is expected of them, the visits are likely to be much more harmonious and fun. The host family should take primary responsibility for the agenda and plans.

Responses to Parenting Behavior

Here are some common disruptive behaviors parents often exercise around their adult children, followed by suggested responses you can try:

Mind-reading. A parent acts as if he is all-knowing—able to tell what you are thinking and feeling as well as discern your opinion without asking you. Typical mind-reading statements are, "I know that you really don't love me. You probably never loved me. You really care more for your father than me. That's unfair because I'm the one who had to do all the parenting."

Generally speaking, the mind-reader fears relationships and uses this technique to cause his own children to reject him. He is suspicious that no one accepts him, so, in order to ward off the pain of being rejected by his children, he uses this technique to push his children away from him.

The net effect of mind-reading is that it causes adult children to distance themselves from their parents. Adult children may be tempted to defend or explain their positions. Sometimes they explode due to the frustration of their parents' mind-reading endeavors.

There are several positive ways to respond to parents who try to read your mind. First, try to see the action as your parent's attempt to make contact with you. Simply say, "Dad, it seems that you are really trying to get close—almost like you are inside my head. I appreciate the interest, but I would prefer that you just ask me how I feel and what I think instead of telling me what you think I feel and think."

Second, do not respond at all. Look at your parent for a few seconds and continue what you were doing when he or she made the statement. If mind-reading continues, maintain silence. When you have a chance, change the subject.

The worst thing to do is to engage the mind-reader in conversation by responding directly to his comments. If he says, "You really prefer not to be here, don't you?" don't say, "Dad, that is just not true. You know I want to be here." Try this instead: "Do you and God have something in common—the ability to read minds?"

Negativism, complaining, and self-pity. Parents sometimes are suspicious of others' motives and tend to see the glass half empty instead of half full. Singing a song of woe about everything keeps them going. They may complain about the loud telephone, the government, and the disrespect of children today for their parents.

Self-pity is used to get attention or to keep the adult children in line. This parent feels inadequate and unable to change things except by way of complaining. Parental complaints and self-pity are attempts to provoke guilt in the adult child, which is then used to whip the adult child into shape. For example: "It's just not fair, Charles. You expect us to take care of you and your family. We ought to get a little respect as your parents. You didn't used to be this way, Charles. We've been nice to you; what did we do to deserve this? We are your parents, Charles; you shouldn't treat us this way."

The first response to such behavior is to try the direct approach. Say something like, "Mom, is there something you want to accomplish by all this complaining? If so, tell me what it is and I will try to cooperate." Another direct response is "Mom, I don't feel bad about your complaint and I promise I will resist all temptations to feel guilty. I care too much for our relationship to let myself get tricked into doing something for you because I feel bad. I want to cooperate with you because you make an honest request of me, not because you have nagged me into it."

When a parent continues to complain, simply remove yourself from the situation by changing the subject, leaving the room, or ignoring him. Do not reward complaining and negative behavior by paying attention to it.

Hysteria. The hysteric parent makes mountains out of molehills by overreacting to events. For example, the adult child moves away and the parent sees it as an overwhelming problem. He might say, "I'll probably never see you again. You are also going to destroy my relationship with my grandchildren."

Respond to the hysteric parent by saying, "You seem very concerned about our relationship. Do you have any suggestions? Are you saying that we, as two families, cannot adapt to this move? Are you getting pleasure from telling me how bad this move will be on everyone?"

You may confront a persistently hysteric parent with overexaggeration and say, "Yes, you are right. This move will be the absolute worst event that has ever happened to us. It is the end, no doubt. We'll never be able to handle this, nor will you. This family is not strong enough or committed enough. After all, we are only your children and your grandchildren."

A more direct and gentle approach may be, "Are you feeling a little insecure or anxious about not seeing us as much? Yes, it will be different for all of us, but I am willing to work with it, are you?"

Faultfinding, put-downs and criticizing. Parents with these traits are usually very outward, boisterous, harsh, and to the point. They take potshots at their children without basis. Maybe they believe that the way to motivate people is by telling them what is wrong with them. Generally this behavior produces a hostile, irritable, and combative family environment. Put-down artists might use these statements: "Every time I invite you and your kids over, you are never here on time"; or "If you don't start sitting on those kids a little bit more they are going to turn out just like you."

In response to the faultfinding parent, you could say, "Dad, I know that this may surprise you, but what I have heard you say in the last few minutes sounds full of criticism. I am tired of it and it does not motivate me. In fact, I resist it."

Or try a statement like this: "Look, I want to have a good time with you and I want us to get along. But I am finding it very difficult to get along because I'm feeling criticized. If you want to continue criticizing, I can't stop you. But I will not go along with it either. If you keep it up I'll either leave the room or stop talking to you. I will not participate in our relationship in this way. You are too important to me. I do not have to be put down in order to be motivated or corrected."

A third response is: "Mom, how can I tell you that your fault-finding really bugs me? I feel like leaving. I would like to think that we've grown beyond motivating each other by using criticism."

Smothering. A smothering parent is the one who approves of you as long as you are doing what he thinks you ought to be doing and in the way he thinks you ought to be doing it. Sometimes they are saintly, very helpful, and self-sacrificing which, they believe, gives them the right to smother you with their expectations.

It is tricky to deal with the smothering parent because his actions appear somewhat innocent. For example, the parent comes up to you or one of your children and says, "I love you and that's why I say some of the things I do." This means you are to overlook her behavior, appreciate her motives, and say, "Well, Mom, I love you too." Smothering is a manipulative ploy that strives for a contrived closeness. How can the adult child not respond to a direct "I love you" from a parent?

Respond to a smothering parent by saying, "Thank you, Mom, for telling me that you love me." Do not pursue it any further than that. Such a response disciplines the parent in her expectations of you.

You may also say, "Mom, I appreciate what you had to say. However, I feel pressured right now. I do care for you very much. But I need to show it when I feel like it, not when I've been prompted. Don't you agree?"

Hidden agendas. Some parents are like icebergs. On the surface everything is fine. But below the surface there are hidden agendas and subtle conditions which are not always clear and sometimes they change the rules of their relationship with you and you don't know it. When you ask, "What's wrong?" the parent will respond with, "Nothing." Obviously the "nothing" is not true. Further, it is the bait trying to hook you into figuring out what the parent keeps hidden.

When you become aware that a parent is upset about something, simply ignore the signals. Don't take the bait and ask him, "What's wrong?" Go on as if nothing is wrong. This may cause him to deal with it internally or bring it to the surface and be more honest with you about the problem.

If you cannot resist the temptation to ask what's wrong, then go ahead; but do so simply. Once your parent tells you the problem, thank him and tell him you will think about it or consider it. You could also ask the parent for some specific suggestions. His responses will help you know what he or she expects and will clarify the rules of the game. Ask your parent to be specific so that there are no misunderstandings. Say, "Mom, I understand this upsets you. If I do it another way you will be less bothered, is that correct?"

Helpful Source Materials

Chapters 2-8

1. *Psychotherapy and Growth*, by W. Robert Beavers, M.D. New York: Brunner/Mazel Publishers, 1977.

2. *No Single Thread: Psychological Health in Family Systems*, by Jerry M. Lewis, W. Robert Beavers, John Gosset, and Virginia Austin Phillips. New York: Brunner/Mazel, 1976.

3. *Families and Family Therapy*, by Salvador Minuchin. Cambridge: Harvard University Press, 1974.

4. *Families: What Makes Them Work*, by David H. Olson and Hamilton I. McCubbin. Beverly Hills, CA: Sage Publications, 1983.

5. *Marriage Personalities*, by David Field. Eugene, OR: Harvest House Publishers, 1986.

Chapter 9

1. *Adult Children of Alcoholics*, by Janet Geringer Woititz. Pompano Beach: Health Communications, Inc., 1983.

Chapter 10

1. *Surviving the Breakup: How Children Actually Cope with Divorce*, by Judith S. Wallerstein and Joan B. Kelly. New York: Basic Books, 1980.

2. *The Single Parent*, by Virginia Watts. Old Tappan, NJ: Fleming H. Revell, 1976.

3. "Children of Divorce as Adults," by Calvin Rubenstein. *Psychology Today*, January, 1980 (pp. 74-75).

Chapters 12-13

1. *Expository Dictionary of New Testament Words*, by W.E. Vine. Westwood: Fleming H. Revell, 1966.

2. "Personal Authority Via Termination of the Intergenerational Hier-archial Boundary: A New Stage in the Family Life Cycle, by Donald Williamson. *Journal of Marital and Family Therapy*, October, 1981.

3. "Contextual Family Therapy," by I. Boszormenyi-Nagy and G. Spark. In *Handbook of Family Therapy*, A. Gurman and D. Kniskern (eds.). New York: Brunner/Mazel, 1981.

4. "Family of Origin as a Therapeutic Resource for Adults in Marital and Family Therapy: You Can and Should Go Home Again," by James L. Framo. *Family Process*, June, 1976.

Chapter 14

1. *Your Child's Self Esteem*, by Dorothy Briggs. Garden City, NJ: Double-day and Company, Inc., 1970.

2. "Stepfamilies: The Restructuring Process" in *Marriage and Divorce Today*, Vol. 8, Number 40, May 9, 1983.

3. "Living in a Blended Family," by Neil Kuyper. *Marriage Encounter*, August, 1981.

Other Good Harvest House Reading

MARRIAGE PERSONALITIES
by *David Field*

Take a fresh look at marriage and its seven distinct personalities. Valuable information about marriage, new insights into your spouse's behavior, and an increased ability to give and receive deeper dimensions of love and joy.

TEENAGERS: PARENTAL GUIDANCE SUGGESTED
by *Rich Wilkerson*

With dynamic impact, well-known youth speaker Rich Wilkerson has captured for every sincere parent the secrets of achieving a fulfilling relationship with his teen. Honest answers for the tough issues we face with our children. Formerly *Hold Me While You Let Me Go*.

MORE HOURS IN MY DAY
by *Emilie Barnes*

There can be more hours in your day when you use the collection of calendars, charts, and guides in this useful book on home time management.

PARENTHOOD WITHOUT HASSLES—Well Almost
by *Kevin Leman*

You will find this book to be practical in every sense of the word. Its aim is to teach parents how to better understand themselves and their children and how to create situations in the home conducive to Christian growth and learning.

STRESS IN THE FAMILY
How to Live Through It
by *Tim Timmons*

Inner and outer stress factors can destroy you and your family! Understanding the pressure you tolerate daily, you will discover *action-steps* that use stress to build you up rather than break you down.

PARENTS: TALK WITH YOUR CHILDREN
by *V. Gilbert Beers*

One of life's most intimate human relationships is that of parent and child. Nothing is more important for a parent than knowing how to reach the heart of his or her child. Nothing is more important for a child than having parents who share their hearts.

V. Gilbert Beers, father of five and bestselling author of *Little Talks About God and You*, shares his experiences and insights and challenges parents to develop the kind of *talking relationship* with their children that will bring a lifelong friendship.

Dear Reader:

We would appreciate hearing from you regarding this Harvest House nonfiction book. It will enable us to continue to give you the best in Christian publishing.

1. What most influenced you to purchase *Family Personalities*?
   ☐ Author   ☐ Recommendations
   ☐ Subject matter   ☐ Cover/Title
   ☐ Backcover copy   ☐ _____

2. Where did you purchase this book?
   ☐ Christian bookstore   ☐ Grocery store
   ☐ General bookstore   ☐ Other
   ☐ Department store

3. Your overall rating of this book:
   ☐ Excellent   ☐ Very good   ☐ Good   ☐ Fair   ☐ Poor

4. How likely would you be to purchase other books by this author?
   ☐ Very likely   ☐ Not very likely
   ☐ Somewhat likely   ☐ Not at all

5. What types of books most interest you?
   (check all that apply)
   ☐ Women's Books   ☐ Fiction
   ☐ Marriage Books   ☐ Biographies
   ☐ Current Issues   ☐ Children's Books
   ☐ Self Help/Psychology   ☐ Youth Books
   ☐ Bible Studies   ☐ Other _____

6. Please check the box next to your age group.
   ☐ Under 18   ☐ 25-34   ☐ 45-54
   ☐ 18-24   ☐ 35-44   ☐ 55 and over

Mail to: Editorial Director
Harvest House Publishers
1075 Arrowsmith
Eugene, OR 97402

Name _____

Address _____

City _____ State _____ Zip _____

Thank you for helping us to help you in future publications!